T0317032

First Writings

Jacques Lacan

First Writings

Translated by Russell Grigg

polity

Polity Press
65 Bridge Street
Cambridge CB2 1UR, UK

Polity Press
111 River Street
Hoboken, NJ 07030, USA

ISBN-13: 978-1-5095-6130-8 – hardback

A catalogue record for this book is available from the British Library.

Library of Congress Control Number: 2024936691

Typeset in 11.5 on 14 pt Adobe Garamond Pro by
Cheshire Typesetting Ltd, Cuddington, Cheshire
Printed and bound in Great Britain by CPI Group (UK) Ltd, Croydon

For further information on Polity, visit our website:
politybooks.com

Contents

Translator's Note vii

Foreword by Jacques-Alain Miller ix

Abasia in a Woman Traumatized by War 1

Simultaneous Madness 11

Structure of the Paranoiac Psychoses 23

'Inspired' Writings: Schizography 45

The Problem of Style and the Psychiatric Conception of Paranoiac Forms of Experience 75

Motives of Paranoiac Crime: The Papin Sisters' Crime 81

Psychology and Aesthetics 93

Hallucinations and Delusions 105

References 113

Translator's Note

The present translations of early articles by Lacan, published between 1928 and 1935, follow the terminology current in the day and also retain the technical language of medicine and psychiatry as it appears in the original articles.

References to Freud's work are to *The Standard Edition of the Complete Psychological Works of Sigmund Freud*, in 24 volumes published by Hogarth Press and the Institute of Psycho-Analysis, London.

All text in square brackets has been added by the translator.

Franck Rollier gave very helpful advice on the translation and Kerry Murphy generously read an entire draft of the manuscript. That said, any errors of translation are mine alone.

Foreword 9

Jacques-Alain Miller

Before he became an analyst, Lacan was a psychiatrist. The articles in the present collection would not be being republished if they didn't invite us to read them retroactively. What can they teach us about the formation of this future analyst who would go on to turn his discipline upside down in the 1950s?

First, I would highlight that his clinical approach is rooted in the uniqueness of each case. Cases are not chosen for being typical, but rather for their 'singularity'. Each one must necessarily present an 'original character' or be 'atypical'. One might recognize from the outset an orientation towards the 'one-by-one' required by the practice of psychoanalysis. Lacan's thesis in medicine takes the form of a monograph of this kind.

The singularity of each case is found at the level of the clinical details. They are studied with a concern for precision that extends down to the smallest minutiae, to the point where the observation may seem labyrinthine to the reader. Lacan will later declare his taste for 'fidelity to the symptom's formal envelope'.

Regarding his strictly psychiatric training, Lacan speaks of his debt solely to Clérambault, who is the object of homage on a scale that would seem to indicate that the master had a claim on his pupil. Be that as it may, once Lacan had left the orbit of his master, he nonetheless pays tribute in his review,

10 'Psychology and Aesthetics', to the feature of 'mental automatism', initially discovered and named as such by Clérambault, as a structural entity. Lacan will say nothing different in 1966.

Three other traits carry traces of the future. There is the use of the word 'structure' to refer to the organization of an entity that forms a whole, separate from other entities, and detached from the concept of development (initially in 'Structure of the Paranoiac Psychoses'). There is the importance given to the analysis of the writings of patients, as we see in particular in '"Inspired" Writings: Schizography'. And then, from there, there is the related connection established between symptoms and literary creations.

I won't go any further into the detail of these effects of deferred action, the tendency to find this 'already there' being nothing but an illusion (cf. *Écrits*, 53).

With the exception of two reviews, the two articles referred to above plus his thesis mark the highpoint of Lacan's output intended primarily for psychiatrists. The texts that follow on style and on the Papin sisters appeared in *Le Minotaure*, a literary journal linked to the milieu of the surrealists, whose interest had already been aroused by the thesis. With 'Inspired Writings', Lacan will begin referring to Breton, Éluard and Péret.

The series of what I have called his 'First Writings' ends here. It was a question of making a selection. I judged that the more technical psychiatric works of the 1920s were not liable to throw light on the path taken by Lacan's thought, nor that they would interest the public any more than the psychiatry of today. They cannot be considered 'writings' in the strict sense.

Lacan began his analysis in 1932. He subsequently writes as an analysand, then as an analyst. From the outset he plans to contribute something new and to enter his career with a splash.

11 The 'something new' was the first version of the mirror stage in 1936. He attended the International Psychoanalytical

Congress in Marienbad and presented the discovery that turned out to be the starting point of his revolutionary teaching. In terms of making a 'splash', he was cut off after ten minutes by Ernest Jones, who was chairing the session. So much for that! He harboured resentment over it for years to come.

The same year, it is as a Freudian that he expressed himself in a work he considered 'fundamental'. He does not hesitate to criticize Freud for having been unfaithful to the phenomenology of [analytic] experience by losing his way in his theory of the 'reality principle', which Lacan resolved to take psychoanalysis beyond. The mirror stage, which was discovered and formalized shortly after, cut short [*couper les ailes*] this new development.

On publishing his *Écrits* in 1966 Lacan dates the same year, 1936, as the moment of his 'entry into psychoanalysis'. Two years later, a masterful text was already proposing to re-establish psychoanalysis – not on the primacy of signifiers, but on the broader concept of a 'complex', only one aspect of which had been perceived by Freud. The result did not rise to the level of his ambitions; these were finally realized in 1951 with 'The Rome Report'.

Authors. Several articles list more than one author. However, Lacan considered himself to be their sole author (personal communication).

Collaborators on this publication 12

Coordination by Guy Briole.

Pénélope Fay was responsible for editing the texts, with Anne Brunet, Geneviève Cloutour-Monribot, Judith Couture, Françoise Kovache, Patricia Loubet, Bérengère Nicolas, Lise Roullet, Anne Semaille and Vanessa Sudreau.

Abasia in a Woman Traumatized by War 13

PUBLISHED IN *REVUE NEUROLOGIQUE DE PARIS*, 1928*

We present this case because of the singularity of a motor disturbance probably pithiatic in nature. Concussed during the war on 22 June 1915 by the explosion of a shell that fell on a neighbour's house and destroyed her own, and having received a number of superficial injuries herself, the patient has progressively formed a motor syndrome, the most remarkable expression of which can be observed when she walks.

The patient withdraws by walking backwards on tiptoes, slowly at first and then hurriedly. She interrupts these steps at regular intervals with several complete rotations executed in a counter-clockwise direction, that is, from right to left. We will return to the details of this way of walking that is – we say this now – unaccompanied by any neurological signs of an organic nature.

The patient's history is difficult to ascertain owing to the inexhaustible and disorganized verbiage with which the patient strives, it would seem, to overwhelm the doctor from the beginning of the interview: dramatic complaints, pathogenic interpretations ('her entire left side had collapsed into her 14
coccyx', etc., etc.) and a history in which dates are confused and greatly disordered.

* Co-authors MM. Trénel and Jacques É.-L. Lacan.

We managed to determine the following facts, however.

On 22 June 1915, in Saint-Pol-sur-Mer, an artillery shell from a 380[mm gun] destroyed three houses, including her own. When she was uncovered, her left leg was trapped in the collapsed floor. She obligingly describes the extraordinarily contorted position into which she was thrown by the blast. She was transported to the Saint-Paul de Béthune hospital where they discovered shrapnel wounds, superficial wounds on her scalp, her nose, the right thoracic wall and the right supraspinatus fossa.

The motor sequelae of a concussive order subsequently continued to be apparent, for in every account she emphasized the words that the officer said to her, 'Stand up straight, you will stand up straight, you are straight, stay straight.' Her psychotherapy, which began thus, was and remained ineffective, assuming that it did not give her a nosocomial education.

Following brief stays in a number of local hospitals, she arrived in Paris in August 1915. Only the wound on her back had not healed; it was suppurating. It was impossible to learn from her exactly when the wound healed – September at the latest, it would seem. But from that period her gait affected a pseudo-contracture on tiptoes; she walked forwards; and she suffered from back pain, but could stand upright. She claimed that her right arm, which was swollen, as it is now, was paralysed.

Her history in the following years comprises a long list of
15 hospitalizations, consultations with doctors, convalescent residencies, and then, from May 1920, endless quarrels with invalid centres with which she continues to be in conflict. She resided successively in la Salpêtrière, Laennec, an American clinic, and Saint-Louis, where she received scarifications in the cervical region which seem to have stimulated the surfacing of small fragments of shrapnel and shreds of fabric. She then entered the service of the duc de Choiseul as a maid, a position that her

crises, clearly pithiatic in appearance, and the obvious eccentricity of her gait soon obliged her to leave.

Her gait effectively changed in appearance several times: walking by taking tiny steps, which the patient calls 'by boat'; then walking in the manner of children who 'make dust'; and lastly crossing her legs in front of her one after the other as she walked. It was then, in January 1923, that she was admitted to Laennec, and quickly discharged before she thought she was ready. It was right at the time she was obliged to leave her bed against her will that she started walking backwards.

In 1923 she was seen by M. Souques at la Salpêtrière. It seems that at that time the walking backwards was already made more complicated by initially doing half-turns and then, later, full-turns. She was given electric shock treatment but to no avail.

M. Lhermitte observed her in 1924, and his observations, which he kindly shared with us, helped us to study the patient's history, which has broadly speaking remained unchanged since.

During this entire period, she consulted numerous doctors,
attaching utmost importance to every step she took. Once, 16
when jostled in the street by a lout, she suffered from a 'collapsed thorax'; later, when jostled by a policeman, she spent two days 'with her left eye open, unable to close it', etc.

In M. Lhermitte's unit, she would walk backwards without spinning round, except when she was getting into bed at nighttime. The gait with its spinning reappeared when *in May* 1927 she was admitted to Sainte Anne as a result of mental troubles that first appeared in February 1927: auditory hallucinations, waves of reproach over the way she has spent her life; and 'she even blocked up her chimney to stop these waves from coming in', 'someone got her pregnant without her knowledge with two dead foetuses; it was a doctor who was sending her these waves', as she wrote to the governor of Les Invalides, threatening to set fire to his house.

This polymorphous hallucinatory delusion with hallucinations of hearing and general sensitivity eased during her stay in our unit.

Motor symptoms. – The patient walked in the manner we have described, walking backwards making full circles as she went. These circles were spaced out when the patient had reasonably long distances to cover. She multiplied them, on the contrary, when she moved about in a confined space – for example, from the chair where she was being examined to the bed on which she was asked to lie down. She stated that walking like this was necessary for her to stand upright, and if anyone tried to convince her to walk forwards, she would adopt a strange stance, with her head buried between her shoulders, her right shoulder higher than the left, would cry and moan, saying that everything was 'collapsing into her thorax'. She would then advance painfully with her foot turned inwards, placing her foot too far
17 out in front, cross her legs, then, as soon as she was no longer being observed, assume her rapid gait with small hurried steps, on tiptoes, and progress backwards.

If one insisted and, taking her by the hand, attempted to get her to walk forwards, she would bend double, adopting a stance reminiscent of camptocormia, then let herself fall to the ground or even collapse – an act that would occasionally be accompanied by very loud protests and groans of pain.

An orderly confirmed to us that she had seen her walk normally for several metres when she thought she was alone and unobserved.

Absence of any symptoms of the cerebellar series.

There is no protrusion or deformation of the vertebral column.

No apparent muscular atrophy in the muscles, neck, back, lumbar region, or in the upper or lower limbs. No contracture or segmental hypotonia in the movement of limbs or head. The loss of muscular strength in active movement observable in the upper limbs in, for instance, the act of shaking hands is so pronounced (accompanied moreover by subjective pain in the interscapular region) that it is considered pithiatic, if not voluntary.

Examination of the teguments. – A star-shaped, irregular scar the size of a two-franc piece [27mm] forming an adherent depression can be observed at the external angle of the right scapula. At the base of the right hemithorax along the axillary line, a linear and slightly keloidal scar, 6cm long. On the left side and lobule of the nose, a fairly deep scar. Lastly, in the frontoparietal region of the scalp, almost along the median line, a bluish linear scar 3½cm in length, slightly adherent in depth.

Lastly, in the two periparotid regions, one can observe two 18
indurated lumps on the posterior edge of the masseters, in front of the earlobes, the one on the right smaller and non-adherent to the skin under which it moves, and the larger one on the left adhering to the skin at the level of a small star-shaped scar that the patient attributed to the scarifications performed on her at Saint-Louis in 1921.

A *local oedema* can be readily observed visually and by palpitation at the level of the right forearm which appears clearly swollen in comparison with the left forearm. A hardened oedema, the subdermal tissue appearing thicker when palpitated, the fineness of the skin unchanged, no cyanosis, no thermic disturbance. Measurements taken at the level of the upper third of the forearm gave a circumference of 28cm on the right and 24 on the left. This strictly local oedema, *which does not extend to either the [upper] arm or hand*, had already been observed by M. Souques.

Sensitivity. – The patient complains of severe subjective pains in the posterior cervical region and in the interscapular region. The slightest touch in the region from the last cervical vertebra down to the 5th dorsal [vertebra] provokes screams, violent protest and a refusal to be examined.

Examination of her objective sensitivity (tactile and thermal) displays no disturbance in her, apart from completely capricious hypoaesthesia that varies with each examination. M. Lhermitte noted: total analgesia of the entire tegument. Awareness of body position is normal.

Reflexes. – The patellar and Achilles tendon reflexes are normal. The triceps is weak. The brachioradialis and the cubito- and radio-pronator are very brisk.

19 Cutaneous plantar reflexes: normal on the right, extremely weak on the left, normal in flexion. Abdominal reflexes, normal.

Pupillary accommodation and light reflexes are normal. No other sensory disturbance.

Labyrinth examination. – We now turn to the labyrinthine examination.

M. Halphen was kind enough to conduct this examination. He observed:

Barany test: At 35″ [seconds], classic nystagmus with direction varying according to the position of the head.

Rotation test: (10 rotations in 20″). The patient collapsed, could not be held up, cried out loud and was unable to be set back on her feet.

This hyperreflexia is only observed in *pithiatics* (or in certain cerebral centres without lesions). Moreover, in repeating the test, we were not able to obtain a nystagmic reflex (5 to 11″ maximum instead of 40″).

This dissociation between the rotation test and the caloric test cannot be explained.

Following the rotation [test], the patient was able to take several steps forward.

This test could not be repeated because of the excessive response it produced in the patient.

It was the same for the voltaic examination that M. Baruk was kind enough to perform. However, despite the difficulties of the examination, he observed a normal reaction (inclination of the head in the direction of the positive pole at 3½ amps) accompanied by the usual sensations, but greatly exaggerated by the patient who let herself slide to the ground.

Moreover, every physical examination or therapeutic endeav- 20
our is met with an excessive response, energetic protest and attempts to avoid the examination; nothing more than a simple examination of her patellar reflex will cause the patient to claim that it has produced a swelling of the knee.

It goes without saying that there was no question of a lumbar puncture, which would have inevitably provided a material basis for new demands.

The x-ray of the skull performed by M. Morel-Kahn was negative.

Nothing can give a better idea of the patient's mental state than the letter she addressed in 1924 to one of the doctors who had observed her.

> Dear Doctor,
>
> The woman who walks backwards sends her respects and owes you an apology for not having stayed in touch.
>
> In September I went to Britanny (Morbihan), the air and the sun did me a lot of good but 24 days were not enough for me, having, since the end of June 1923, redone backwards all the nervous movements of bombardments, air currents and impossible balance.
>
> I no longer dare go out alone, I no longer have any strength, and I lower my head as I walk backwards. Moving my right arm, as before the violence towards me in the street, the weakening of the left side, makes me pull my left leg out straight; I cross going backwards for a moment, and one day I managed the three floors with my left heel in the air, the end of my foot maintaining this walk, perilous and without any way to disengage it, it would break. I have fallen into

the bottom of cars or taxis several times. I go out as little as possible under these conditions, but my head needs a lot of air.

21 Mr X. . ., lawyer at the Court of Appeal, is going to represent me at the Pensions Tribunal around the beginning of next month. It's quite long, and am very weakened by these blows and brutalities, movements that I would not have repeated and internally broke the little that kept me upright. My thorax still wrapped in a sheet, I am completely bent over, without thereby walking twisted towards the heart and around the head, so I no longer try, it is empirical. According to whether I move my head, I stay with my mouth open as well as contraction, if I forget to stay upright.

If I could feel peaceful in the open air, apart from the cold, these inconveniences that had left me would cease perhaps. I had called for help following the displacement of air, while waiting for my father's complaints. In conclusion, the nerves are withdrawing, others doesn't function and no way to rest on my heels. I would have come, dear Doctor, and pay my respects to you and to the Professor as well, but I have such difficulties. Please accept my best wishes.

M. SOUQUES – I do indeed recognize M. Trénel's strange patient. I observed her at La Salpêtrière in January 1923 with my intern, Jacques de Massary. At the time she presented with the same problems as today: an exaggerated way of walking and an oedema on the upper right limb.

She would sometimes walk on tiptoes, at others on the sides of her feet while she waddled from side to side. Sometimes she would walk backwards, rotating as she went, etc. According to her, walking on tiptoes was due to the pain in her heels and walking like a duck to the pains in her back (where there were scars from her injuries). But it is obvious that the other ways of walking were not at all to relieve the pain.

As to the oedema on the upper right limb, it was limited to the lower part of the arm and forearm. The hand remained
untouched. It was white and soft. She attributed this to having 22
been violently thrown against the wall 'like a doormat'. The unusually segmented nature of this oedema made us think it was factitious, but we found no trace of constriction or compression of the limb.

At the time, the patient did not present any litigious ideas. The diagnosis recorded: accident neurosis.

M. G. ROUSSY – Like M. Souques, I recognize this patient that I examined at length in my unit at the Paul-Brousse hospice, with my friend Lhermitte. At the time, we considered her a classic case of war psychoneurosis with grotesque and burlesque manifestations that developed on top of an underlying intellectual disability. Moreover, the patient carried around with her a war pensioner's booklet and did not disguise her intention to obtain an increase in the percentage of her pension. We suggested to the patient that she be hospitalized with a view to an extended examination in psychotherapeutic treatment. But 48 hours after entering the unit, and before the treatment had even commenced, the patient left the hospital without being discharged.

This small fact confirms the opinion of MM. Trénel and Lacan and highlights the particular mental state of this patient, similar to so many that we have seen during the war.

Simultaneous Madness 23

PUBLISHED IN *ANNALES MÉDICO-PSYCHOLOGIQUES*, 1931*

We present to the S.M.P. [Société médico-psychologique] two cases of *délire-à-deux* whose novelty, we believe, resides in their almost complete autonomy, including an element of mutual criticism.

They differ in this respect from the classic doctrine which stresses 'mental contagion' and is based on cases where one can clearly detect an inducing and an induced delusion, which abates once it is distanced from the former.

1st case of '*délire-à-deux*' – *Mother and daughter Rob. . .*

The mother (Marie-Joséphine), 70 years of age.

Interpretative syndrome with panic attacks. Auditory hallucinations, oneiric in nature and predominantly hypnagogic. Visual elements of a palpably confusional type. Persistence, variable over the course of evolution, of post-oneiric delusional elements. – Reactions: calls for help, accuses herself of imaginary acts, corrects, apologizes. Disorderly, transitory acts. – Amnesic confabulations. – Evolving over more than a year.

* Co-authors MM. Henri Claude, P. Migault and J. Lacan.

Insomnia, whose recent easing corresponds to the easing of other symptoms.

24 Emotional shock (death of her son a year ago), coinciding with the beginning of the development of her morbidity. Possible traces of endotoxicity and exogenous intoxication probable.

When interviewed, the patient adopts an affable, kindly attitude, free of any hint of paranoia, at times gently reticent.

Over the course of the various interviews that we have had with her, she states:

'People enter her house with a copied key, they search, they rob her and they take her money; she cannot, however, categorically affirm this. It is a matter of small objects of little value. "It is, as it were, for the pleasure of taking."'

'People are spreading gossip about her in the neighbourhood. There is clearly madness in it all; you would have to be a bit crazy to be so nasty; there's jealousy of one's health in it.'

'The suppliers and the neighbours give her poisoned food. (She frequently throws it into the bin without touching it, hence considerable waste observed on investigation.) She gives an extra two francs to get "good quality"'.

'Several voices speak to her out of thin air. They claim she killed her son. They speak to her through the wall: "Be careful, you are surrounded by bad people. You are surrounded by machines that report on everything that happens at your place."'

'She is being observed constantly with the help of a set of mirrors to the point where she has had to cover the mirror over the fireplace.'

She cannot wash, 'she is always being watched'. Old tunes [*scies*] in the tick-tock of her alarm clock. Bad tastes, bad smells.

25 Mental condition: lucid. Retention of acquired knowledge. Mental arithmetic quite good. Retention of elementary logic.

Physical examination: slight tremor of the hand on entry, tachycardia, blood pressure 23/13kpa [172/97mmHg] on Pachon [oscillometer]. Azotemia 0.27. Remarkable absence of canities. Ungual dystrophy of the right digitus medius. No oculo-pupillary disorders. Tendon reflexes normal. Caffeinism detected and perhaps ancillary alcoholism. Humoral reactions, blood and CSF, negative.

The daughter (Marguerite-Marie), 35 years of age, employee of Crédit Lyonnais.

Atypical interpretative psychosis. Appearance is sthenic, emotional and sullen. An autism that renders her complaints barely coherent hides behind her reticence. At the outset declares some bizarre practices of an imaginative nature that are the very same ones which, admitted to with certainty, serve as the basis of her interpretations. Their puerility makes her subject to ridicule.

Partial relationship with a barely coherent erotomanic theme.

She is more particularly bitter towards her work colleagues since the death of her brother, 'who did not even put a stop to their mocking ways'.

Auditory illusions: manifest discordance between their content and the allusive signification she attributes to them.

Prides herself on an attitude that is systematically arrogant and distant. Inquiries reveal minimal external displays; in the office she is regarded as normal. Autistic intellectual activity.

Her affections are mainly towards her mother. But, in their life together, strange behaviour is revealed, despotism exercised by the daughter with episodes of brutality.

Expresses herself in a low, reticent and hostile voice: 'It has 26
brought her a lot of pain . . . Her mother has not seen her laugh
for ages . . . The continual mocking has left her in a state',
etc.

We finally obtain a fact from her: one of her colleagues, C. H., brilliant speaker at gatherings, appears to have inspired in her feelings for him, at least a preoccupation with him, which has apparently led her to write the following words on small pieces of paper: 'C. H. married', 'C. H. not married', 'C. H. sweet', 'C. H. nasty', 'C. H. monster', etc. These pieces of paper apparently fell into the hands of an employee of the bank; she thinks that since then she can recognize all kinds of allusions to these displays 'that don't go with my age; there is an age at which one should not have ideas that are overly naïve'.

Also, naïve drawings, a Virgin, a Christ at play, a woman carrying a child on her head – it seems it was all discovered and caused amusement.

Clear auditory illusions: while drawing a Christ, she pronounced these words: 'fat arse' [*gros pétard*]. She connects to the same theme – we couldn't find out why – disagreeable allusions to relations she says she has with a movie actor, Marius M. 'Many times I have heard, "Marius and a hundred thousand francs", I can confirm it.'

Palpable irritability when she is smiled at, even kindly.

Permanently worried about her mother's future. Displays strong emotion at the memory of her deceased brother.

Great reader, according to the neighbours. Said to have passed days reading in bed. Recites poetry by heart.

Requested leave last December so as, she says, to take care of her mother. Assisted since then through the kindness of the bank that employed her and would most likely take her back.

27 Rumours of tyranny over her mother and of verbal violence.

Elementary intellectual functions retained, large calculations performed well and rapidly. Physical examination: hypothyroidism, smallness of extremities, 1.46m in height, obesity, hypermastia, pulse 116. Blood pressure 20/11kPa [150/82mmHg] on Pachon [oscillometer]. Pupils react. Tendon reflexes normal. Marked hypersympathicotonia.

Relations between the two delusions. The daughter is an unacknowledged illegitimate child. The mother is said to have had two other children by the same father, one of which was taken into care [*enfants assistés*], and two stillborn twins. Since the son's death, the two women live in isolation, each one the bearer of her own delusion.

The daughter understands exactly her mother's problems, which she explains as 'cerebral anaemia'. She is deeply concerned about her mother's future, has not wanted to force her into a home and asks if she can stay with her in the asylum, should she be required to stay there for any length of time. She declares, deeply offending her mother, that she has observed the disorder of the latter's behaviour on several occasions.

On the other hand, the mother finds unintelligible the irritations that her daughter complains about.

Their shared bedroom is in an extremely squalid state, their budget is entirely consumed by ruinous purchases of food.

The daughter was considered dangerous by their immediate family, whereas the mother, while she names her persecutors – her neighbours, the S.'s – is nevertheless generally treated with kindness owing to her smiling and gracious attitude.

*

2nd case – *The mother and daughter Gol* 28

The mother, Jeanne G., 67 years of age, not committed.

Typical interpretative delusion, developing for at least the past fifteen years. Displays in the street recurring periodically, preceded by certain signs symptomatic in value. House broken into. Ideas of being poisoned. Betrayal by her family and friends. Hostile manifestations often much more demonstrative than efficacious in nature.

Extension of the syndrome, imposing the idea of the subject's limitless notoriety. Reactions: moving house to flee an enemy who cannot be evaded; meaningful interpretations of banal remarks.

Auditory illusions.

Gas.

Electric currents. Feelings of unease that borrow their expression from the vocabularies of electricity, wire coilings, etc.

Reactions: Makes her house draughtproof, stitches up the doors, carries on her person huge bags in which she carries around all her food requirements, seals off holes and corners, stretches out lines of string. ('You would have thought we were in a submarine.') There are certain particularly dangerous corners in these rooms.

Squalor, wastage.

Mental condition undiminished. Moreover: external point of critique preserved: 'Why should I go and complain? I
29 don't have any proof, they would say, "She is just as mad as her daughter who is in Sainte-Anne".' Never any protest in response.

This woman, who is not interned, expresses herself in a very well measured tone, is punctual for meetings that are scheduled for her regarding her daughter, has been supporting her from her own work for some years, and seems to be punctual for work.

Expresses herself in these terms:

'The street is very hostile, lots of people are aware of our history, a large part of the clergy in particular, whose enemies are highly probably the cause of many of our troubles.' 'We Gols. are very well known in Paris, as well known as the president of the Republic.'

Their persecutors come mainly from the world of labourers: 'The other day a man working on the roads said while looking her way: "Hey! Here comes old beefy [*costaud*]!" To which his workmate answered, "Dirty business, that's for sure." – "Dirty business," the other replied. "Who'd have thought we'd be dealing with the likes of such beefy types?"'

The persecution in the street varies in intensity and in kind.

At one point, they couldn't leave the house without someone spitting in their path, 'without being covered in spittle', without being sworn at, 'slut, whore', without being threatened (a tyre blows out, ropes are displayed, black cars locked), or without being laughed at in all kinds of ways.

Regarding her residence, it is constantly being invaded. When they enter her home, 'they leave a mark to show that they have been'. 'They stopped the alarm clock to show what time they came.' 'Initially it was her neighbours, the W's, in collusion with [the telephone company] *Le Matériel Téléphonique*, who carried out these incursions.'

She has often found small signs in her shopping proving that 30
poison was planted in it.

She was given very painful electric currents, primarily in the genital region. She felt a sensation that could only have come from being electrocuted. All these annoyances increased in 1920: in the workshops they were always positioned next to a door where the currents were so strong that the workers would avoid them. The bosses' words gave away the fact that they were making sure that this is how it would be.

Asphyxia, discomfort such that one night in 1925 she and her daughter had to spend the night outside. Olfactory interpretations: scents, etc.

Initially (1917), all the suppliers were scheming to poison her. She was obliged to obtain pharmaceuticals from a place a long way away from her suburb. They have grown weary for the moment.

Negative neurological examination.

Blood pressure 25/13kPa [187/97mmHg]

The daughter, Blanche, 44 years of age.

Paranoid delusion.

Extremely broad construction, which is a second reality – 'the other day', she says, on which another sun shines, a day that she enters when she is fast asleep, and the existence and the events of which are revealed to her by intuition.

These conceptions form a coherent system, constant from one interview to the next. They relate to:

Her body. She is the quadriceph [*quadrucéphale*] with the green eye. What put her onto this was that her blood is scented.
31 At high temperatures, her skin becomes metallic and hardens; then she is a pearl and gives birth to jewels. Her genital parts are unique, as there is a pistil, it is like a flower. Her brain is four times stronger than anyone else's, her ovaries are the most resistant. She is the only woman in the world who does not need to bathe.

On the nature of the sexes, 'when a man bathes, he becomes a lady'. Every lady other than herself needs to bathe, otherwise they are men.

For her, 'there is nothing in her person that is superfluous, there is nothing that needs to be removed'. 'There is nothing in me that needs to be recut, there are no onions to be recut. In me, everything is natural. I do not have a bad desire? I am a lady.'

She is a unique being without an equivalent in the world, who is characterized by:

her successive resurrections: When she dies, she is reduced to ashes from which she is reborn, as is testified by what happened in 1885 and her return to life in 1887 according to papers that are held in the City Hall: the little body that was then withdrawn from her body was subject to all sorts of trials, 'a quadricephalic testing to see if it was strong enough'.

her fertility: She is the mother of all the children born since 1927: 'the quadricephs'.

She can feel their movements in her womb and in her back, she carries them between 27 months and 30 months so that their organs are stronger.

'What is a mother?' – 'A lady who has bathed and with whom the town hall [*mairie*] has placed a child that has been taken out of my body.'

They are withdrawn from her on the second day, the day 32
the 'quadricephallic' regulations come into effect. It is possible because of her reinforced diaphragm. Her internment here [in the hospital] is going to lead to a reduction in the birth rate, because she henceforth refuses to create, though given the length of her pregnancies it will not be noticed straightaway.

her virginity: while, on 'the other day', she could be raped up to twelve times during the night by the Creator in the form of two intertwined snakes, this night she nevertheless woke up a virgin and she remains a virgin. All of this 'ever since the world began'. She is the unique mother and the eternal virgin.

her correspondence with another unique being who is the Creator. Their power mystically alternates: 'How could she create without him? How could he create without her?' Moreover, while she refers to him as 'He', he is nonetheless 'more lady than all the ladies': 'He is the quadriceph with black eyes, his skin is ivory', etc. They are two unique beings, their blood never mixes.

her sovereignty, her infinity, her universality.

Evolution: According to what she says, in 1920 she and her mother underwent difficult trials, electric currents that acted to strengthen her organs, along with 'rapid heartbeats, tension headaches, irritation and the "killer blow" [*coup du lapin*] they wanted to give her with poisonous food'. But that all stopped completely in 1925 and the 'wire coilings' started, which is the means by which everything that she is has been revealed to her. 'It's the wire coilings that told me, in the tick-tock of my clock', etc.

Reactions: The patient admits to strange practices. She makes a stock with the blood from her period, 'I drink some every day,
33 it is fortifying nourishment'; she arrived at the unit with hermetically sealed flasks, one containing faecal matter, the other urine, wrapped in oddly embroidered cloth.

She has decided to stop work, 'They don't give a shit about me, they at least owe me child support.' 'Even if they refuse, they will always work something out under the table with my mother.'

Nevertheless, helps her mother with the housework very regularly, prepares meals, etc. All these declarations are made with a serene smile, a tone full of certainty and smug satisfaction; her responses are easy, lively, sometimes biting: on her virginity, 'If I don't have an eye down there, I have a finger to see with.' 'Ah, no! That nine-months thing doesn't work with me'; etc. The words 'power', 'property' and 'regulation' return endlessly.

Mental condition: Elementary logic intact, retention of acquired knowledge, oriented, correct information about recent events.

Physical examination: Adiposity, diminished basal metabolism, no neurological signs.

Relations between the two delusional women.

The daughter, her mother's only child, is an unacknowledged illegitimate child, as in the previous case. Even more so than in the previous case, their social isolation is obvious; it dates from childhood.

It seems the mother became delusional first. But the child quickly followed her in her interpretations. They came to agree on the expression of their cenesthopathy, anxieties and attacks of panic and on the organization of their defence systems. As the mother says, 'My daughter was then like a normal person.'

34 However, even back then the mother noted that it was quite odd to hear her daughter complain that her thoughts were being stolen. She herself didn't experience anything similar:

all she could recognize was allusions to her own thoughts in conversations.

Now, she is shattered to see her daughter delusional: 'She has delusions of grandeur.' But she scarcely dares to contradict her because she is afraid of her.

In effect, the daughter reprimands her sharply: 'It's annoying, she persists in thinking I am her little daughter, or in treating me as a person just like any other.' 'But no one asked to understand in the first place.' 'She has struck her mother on occasion.'

Moreover, they sometimes attribute the aggravation of their troubles to one another: the mother 'experiences [electric] currents' when her daughter goes out; the daughter tells her, 'It's you, you sent them to me, you old piece of scum.' The mother imports into her own interpretations the character disturbances of her daughter, which she believes she can see are worse on religious holidays. The daughter, trapped in her metaphysical delusion, makes fun of her mother's interpretations and declares that 'there's no need to take notice of any of that' and 'as to the currents, she can take them, they don't worry her'.

A hint of an old affective ambivalence seems worthy of note: 'We lived as two sisters, two very serious sisters, the two of us.' The daughter's hostility grew the more she disowned her relationship to her mother. She would become affected. When her mother used the [first-person plural] '*nous*': '*Allons nous coucher*', 'Let's go to bed', for example – 'In the singular, not in the plural', was the daughter's riposte, in speaking to me, 'You will never make me live as a couple with my mother.'

To summarize: We can highlight the following in these two 35
cases:

(1) A direct hereditary line with analogous reinforcement of the psychopathological defect [*tare psychopathique*]; (2) social isolation that may have caused the disturbances of affect that one can see materializing; (3) the independent evolution of

their delusions with reciprocal possibilities of criticism, which can be gauged by the degree of preservation of contact with reality [*le réel*].

From the point of view of the analysis and classification of delusions, what is characteristic of the mother in the Gol. group is the intuitive, imposed and limited reasoning of the interpretations, which contrasts with the feeling she has of the difficulty of explaining the system.

The daughter's delusion is interesting for its character of enormous egocentrism and the presence of intuitions of periodic return and recommencement (the successive resurrections) that one often encounters in a certain type of paranoid delusion.

Structure of the Paranoiac Psychoses 37

PUBLISHED IN *LA SEMAINE DES HÔPITAUX DE PARIS*, 1931

HISTORY OF THE GROUP AND THE AIM OF THIS STUDY

The conception of paranoia that inherited both the old monomanias and the somatic foundations of the notion of degeneration grouped together psychopathological states that were actually quite diverse. It did, however, have the advantage of alluding to a non-psychogenic ground or basis for all these states. But progress in the clinical field – Kraepelin, the Italians, Sérieux and Capgras – successively separated it from the paranoid states attached to dementia praecox, from the chronic hallucinatory psychoses, and lastly from the more or less transitory forms of delusion that constitute acute paranoia and which have to be included under various categories such as polymorphous psychotic episodes, mental confusion or pre-dementia states.

Restricted in this way, paranoia tends to be confused today with a notion of character, which, it seems, leads to attempts to derive it from normal psychological functioning.

It is against this tendency that I shall attempt to bring together some reflections.

I shall do so by basing myself on the purely phenomenological concept of the *structure* of delusional states. This concept strikes me as critical:

38 *First, from the nosographical point of view*

Here one can grasp the discontinuity with normal psychology, as well as the discontinuity between the states which, with Professor Claude, who has again compared them with paranoid states in order to define them better, I call paranoiac psychoses.[1]

From the diagnostic point of view

Psychopathologies, even those at the limits of normal psychic function, do not display any less rigour than other syndromes of pathology in the grouping of their symptoms. They cannot be too closely analysed. For it is precisely the atypical nature of any given case that will inform us about its symptomatic features and enable us to uncover any gross neurological illness, predict a progressive dementia and thereby alter the prognosis of a delusion whose essential nosographic framework is chronicity without dementia.

From the forensic point of view

These structures will seem either irreducible or resolvable, depending on the case. And this must guide the social preven-

[1] Henri Claude, 'Les psychoses paranoïdes', *Encéphale* 20, no. 3 (March 1925): 137–49.

tative measures incumbent on the psychiatrist through the use of detention.

I will examine, in turn, three types of paranoiac psychoses 39
from these three points of view:

- The 'paranoiac constitution'
- Delusions of interpretation
- Delusions of passion

THE 'PARANOIAC CONSTITUTION'

The features of a delusion are already apparent here. Essentially 'ideative' in the old descriptions, for modern psychiatry their basis is in the concept of a disturbance of affectivity. It does not seem that this latter term has to be limited to the life of the emotions or passions. And only the concept of 'reaction to vital situations', recent in biology and quickly taken up by psychiatry, strikes me as sufficiently comprehensive to explain this total, evolving imprint on the person, which the use made of this expression attributes to it on a daily basis.[2]

Be that as it may, the paranoiac constitution is undoubtedly characterized by:

- the subject's deep-seated attitudes towards the external world;
- blocks of ideas whose specific deviations have given certain authors the idea of a kind of intellectual neoplasia or dysgenesis – a formula that has the clinical value of reflecting well the complexion of the paranoiac temperament; and, lastly,

[2] This concept, introduced into biology by von Uexküll, has been used since by numerous authors. For psychiatry, see Kretschmer; in the United States, A. Myers.

40 – reactions by the social milieu that give a no less faithful image of it.

Four cardinal signs have been described, which I will go back over.

I. Pathological overestimation of oneself

There is an imbalance in the value relations that are more or less implicitly established between the ego and the world at every moment of the life of every subject.

And a unilateral and constant imbalance in the sense of self-satisfaction.

Its manifestations extend from pride that is latent in diverse ways to vanity that is much more frequent and readily degenerates into histrionics.

It seems that Montassut insists upon a hint of an intellectual disturbance when comparing this fundamental attitude to types of systematic misrecognition, here a misrecognition of the 'equation $\frac{\text{success}}{\text{pretention}}$'.[3]

II. Mistrust

This is the same attitude reflected in actual relations with the world.

Mistrust is basic and, as it were, the negative of a delusion, the ready-made mould that is opened up by doubt, into
41 which outbursts of emotions and anxiety will rush, and in

[3] M. Lévy-Valensi, on the other hand, portrays this same attitude of pride in the paranoiac in relation to the extremely broad metapsychological concept to which Jules de Gaultier has given the name 'bovarism'.

which intuitions and interpretations will crystallize and delusions solidify.

III. Errors of judgement

This preformed, primary feature of the personality inclines all judgements towards a *system*. It is itself actually a fixed and underdeveloped form of judgement.

A sort of overflowing, of virulence of logical functioning adds to this. Losing themselves endlessly in sophisms and paralogisms, these subjects, in a happy choice of words, profess an 'unhappy love of logic'.

Amongst these 'reasoning madmen' (Sérieux and Capgras), an entire hierarchy arises, from the feebleminded [*débile*] with his absurd constructions to the self-taught or cultivated theoretician who is at ease with abstract ideas. The latter may find a degree of success within the secret limits of his mental horizon: an appearance of rigour, the clear attraction of fundamentally rudimentary ideas and the opportunity to affirm obstinately and without deviation. Should fortune place him in line with events, he may become a reformer of society or sensibilities, or a 'great intellectual'.

IV. Social maladjustment

Constituted thus, the paranoiac lacks all vital flexibility and psychological sympathy. Even in the best of cases in which his tendencies are crowned with success, he does not know how to take advantage of it for his happiness.

In reality, incapable of submitting to any collective disci- 42
pline, even less so to any team spirit, a paranoiac, who on rare occasions may manage to occupy the place of leader, is almost

always an *outlaw*: despised and punished as a schoolboy, a poor soldier, rejected at every turn.

The ambiguity of his moral position is due to the fact that he needs the judgements of others, which he regularly fails to acquire, and that he hungers to be appreciated while all appreciation humiliates him.

Far from being schizoid, he cleaves closely to reality, so closely that he suffers from it cruelly. He knows how to emphasize to the highest degree the hostile potentialities that are one of the components of social relations. Nothing rivals either his flair for detecting their slightest trace or, by an inter-psychological reaction that must not be neglected, his tactlessness at reinforcing their effectiveness by his attitude.

As one can see, beneath these different features one finds a unique reality whose diverse manifestations are closely related. They are the four sides of a single square. In the middle is the 'psychorigidity' that Montassut has so rightly emphasized:[4]

- *psychical*, which contact with the subject reveals right from the outset (*Empfindungsdiagnose*). Sthenic, argumentative, expansive or rilesome and reticent, he reveals himself to be intransigent. While those close to him and the naïve will only learn this at their expense, the experience of a psychiatrist is not misled.
- *motor*, as is clearly revealed by the person's very par-
43 ticular stance: stiff neck, rigid torso, walks awkwardly, and a handwriting that is odd apart from any delusional features.

[4] Marcel Montassut, *La Constitution paranoïaque*, thesis, Paris, 1925 [Vannes: Commelin, 1924].

Accessory signs

On the basis of these premises, certain adventitious features that can be useful for detecting these subjects fit more readily into normal *psychological deduction* and the common psychology of relations.

Some are favourable: an almost constant honesty, a sense of honour that in no way only translates into excessive susceptibility, even though it tends towards resentment and what in eighteenth-century French was called '*pique*'.

Generally speaking, their honourability is never in question: they have the respect of their neighbours.

One finds autodidacts among them and it is easy to understand how autodidacticism, in its most annoying features, finds fertile soil here.

These subjects are familiar with every form of compensation: more or less open revolt, the appeal to posterity and the attitudes of the solitary figure.

It is not uncommon to find in them a love of nature, where these subjects really find they can freely develop – a pantheistic liberation, I would even say, of a delusion that has more or less taken shape.

Lastly, I refer to the 'passionate idealist' type described by Dide.

It seems to me, however, that we should stop short of the 44
imaginative play and reactions that the term 'bovarism', taken here in a clinical sense, refers to in normal life.[5]

[5] Georges Genil-Perrin, *Les Paranoïaques* (Paris: Maloine, 1926).

DELUSIONS OF INTERPRETATION

Masterfully described by Sérieux and Capgras, delusions of interpretation form the second delusional type of paranoiac syndrome that we encounter. They also constitute a second degree in the delusional indications by which one could locate delusions in relation to reality [*le réel*]. They are the positive, the statue that emerges from the mould formed by the state of mistrust, shaped by doubt, of the previous form.

Appealing to 'affective complexes', 'empirical residues' and 'affective logic', Dromard (in the *Journal de psychologie*) described the arc that goes from character to delusional conviction. He did not succeed in bridging the gulf that separates the two structures. Moreover, one does not see these mechanisms clinically. Rather, under the influence of a triggering cause that is frequently hidden and occasionally represented by a toxic episode, an intercurrent illness or an emotional trauma, a kind of precipitation of meaningful elements is produced, initially permeating a mass of incidents that chance brings the subject's way and whose significance is suddenly transfigured for him.

This is the person who remarks that certain gestures in the street indicate that he is being followed, that he is being spied upon, that his thoughts are being read, or that he is being threatened. According to his social rank, a greater or lesser
45 role is played by the neighbour opposite, the people one hears exchanging words through the window in the courtyard, the building supervisor, the work colleague, the boss or the subordinate in the hierarchy.

A delusion of interpretation is a delusion regarding people in the building, in the street or in the community.

Such interpretations are *multiple*, *extensive* and *repeated*. Every incident of daily life, every public event is liable to end up referencing him. And according to the extent of the subject's information, they all do, in fact.

However extensive these interpretations are, they are centripetal, tightly focused on the subject.

They may also be endogenous, that is, based on coenaesthetic sensations – whether abnormal sensations of either an organic or neurasthenic [*névropathique*] origin – or simply normal sensations that the subject's newly oriented attention gives the appearance of being new.

The essential point of the delusional structure appears to be the following: the interpretation comprises a series of quasi-intuitive, quasi-obsessional *primary givens* that no reasoning organization has primitively organized, whether by selection or by grouping. As has been said, it is 'an annelid, not a vertebrate'.[6]

It is on the basis of these specific 'immediate givens' that it is necessary for the dialectical faculty to come into play. However favourable to deviations of logic the paranoiac structure supposes it [the dialectical faculty] to be, it is not without effort that it organizes the delusion, and it seems that it undergoes it more than it constructs it. It is most often led to a construction so complicated as to extend to a kind of absurdity both in extent and in logical deficiencies. The subject is sometimes 46
aware of this feature of it being impossible to defend, despite his personal conviction that is incapable of detaching itself from the elementary facts.

Indeed, one curious thing that it does not occur to the subject to consider is that the threats that become the very fabric of the subject's life have a *purely demonstrative* character and never lead to any action. However serious they may be, they are remarkably ineffective. Moreover, while the scale of the means employed and their practically ubiquitous character impose on the patient the thought that a group such as the police, the

[6] This image is taken from the oral teaching of my master M. G. de Clérambault, to whom I owe so much regarding content and method that, to avoid the risk of plagiarizing, I would have to render homage to him over each of these terms.

Freemasons or the Jesuits are its instrument, he does not hesitate, however, to refer this conduct, as the cause of his ills, to someone of little account, close to and well known to him.

Also, it has to be emphasized that despite the persistence, the unbearable nature and the cruelty of his persecutions, the patient's reaction is often delayed and sometimes remains nonexistent for a long time. Moreover, one must not hasten to speak of conviction in an overly rigorous sense, nor reinforce its foundations through insensitive questioning. It seems it is often a kind of *justificatory construction*, a minimum of rationalization in the absence of which the patient would be unable to expound his primary certainties. Its logical structure will of course be proportional to the intellectual soundness and culture of the patient. It is the interpretative foundation that the examination must uncover and on which the diagnosis is to be based.

Let us summarize its features:

- A network of interpretations, circular in extension;
- Complexity and vague character of the delusion;
47 – Emotion and reactiveness relatively disproportionate, on the side of less;
- Chronicity: the delusion becoming richer in proportion to the material that the patient's daily experience brings him. Conversely, the reduced and torpid character that it usually adopts after a stay in the milieu of an asylum results, excluding possible intellectual decline, from the drying up of these basic elements.

DELUSIONS OF PASSION

Quite different from the above and located in another register, these delusions, owing to the state of *manic sthenia* underlying them, have been compared by de Clérambault to this chronic emotional state, which is where one has been inclined to define passion. It is due to their second, constant characteristic, the *prevailing idea*, that they sit in the etymological framework of paranoia and occupy a place in our study of delusional structures.

Common in impulsive, degenerate, amoral or perverse subjects, and taxed with various personal or hereditary psychopathological defects, these delusions occasionally appear in the territory of paranoiac constitution.

De Clérambault distinguishes three forms:

- litigious delusions, which Sérieux and Capgras had already differentiated from delusions of interpretation;
- erotomania;
- delusions of jealousy. 48

They present only very superficial similarities to delusions of interpretation, even to those in which litigious [*processives*] reactions or jealous content are prevalent.

Analysis reveals an underlying, initial event that carries a disproportionate emotional charge instead of vague interpretations.

On the basis of this event, a delusion develops that expands, certainly, and can feed on interpretations, but only along the axis opened up by the initial event: a delusion in a *sector*, one might say, and not in a network. Selected in this way at the outset, the elements of the delusion are then grouped concentrically, organized in the manner of a well-argued plea, and present a form of inexhaustible virulence.

They are sustained by a *sthenic state* eminently suited to a *passage-à-l'acte*.

When this *passage-à-l'acte* has been formulated, it adopts the character of an obsessive impulse with the particularity, as demonstrated by H. Claude, of being half integrated into the personality in the form of a prevailing idea.

Just as in other obsessions-impulsions, the *passage-à-l'acte* relieves the pressure of the parasitic idea on the subject, and thus, after many hesitations, carrying out the act puts an end to the delusion and clearly reveals the *degenerative impulsiveness* at its base.

Such are the truly indefatigable querulants who bring interminable lawsuits, file appeal after appeal and, unable to attack
49 the judge himself effectively, lash out at the experts assigned to their case. They overwhelm the authorities and the public with factums; as the need arises, they make symbolic gestures intended to draw the attention of the authorities onto them.

While these subjects are also paranoiacs, with their faulty logic, and being well versed in purely formal exercises, they find incredible resources for discovering the detours and byways offered by the labyrinth of the courts.

At the extremes of these delusions, one finds political assassins and magnicides who struggle for years with their murderous project before resolving to carry it out.[7]

He is also the type who, with a hypochondriacal claim against his doctor, murders him.

The same essential features define as a delusion the jealousy of the jealous partner, even if it is warranted by the facts.

In none of these cases is the interpretation ever forced. One does not see it located in the signification of a minor fact being transformed, but, at most, in a single fact being taken in an exemplary sense: a widespread injustice that has come to

[7] Joseph Lévy-Valensi, '"Les crimes passionnels", Rapport au Congrès de Médecine légale de 1931', *Annales de médecine légale, de criminologie et de police scientifique* 11 (1931): 193–285.

have the force of law, or, on the contrary, justice rendered to everyone save the subject, or the general decline of morals, etc.

Similarly, for the hypochondriac who assaults his doctor, it is not the cenesthopathic illness that is attributed to the more or less mysterious influence of the doctor, as the interpreter would do, but the fact that he has not cured him, for which he has to be severely punished.

Nevertheless, the paranoiac disturbance in the etymological sense can be sensed in the very layout of the delusion – and not only in his reactions, which, disproportionate to the harm by 50
which he is motivated, justify to the highest degree the term 'delusion of acts and feelings', but also in the very ideational organization of the delusions.

This has been admirably demonstrated by de Clérambault for the second type of delusion of this group: erotomania.

De Clérambault's erotomanic delusions

This 'paradoxical' ideational organization, which conveys the idea of a pathological hypertrophy of a chronic state of passion, passes through three phases:

- Euphoria,
- Disappointment, rancour [*dépit*],
- Resentment [*rancune*].

It is based on a number of *postulates*:

- the chosen object being almost always socially superior to the subject in some way, the initiative comes from the object;
- the very success of the love is indispensable to the object's perfection;

- the object is free to act on this love, as his preceding commitments are no longer valid; and
- universal sympathy is attached to the twists and turns, and successes, of this love.

These postulates develop in the face of the facts into thoughts
about the *paradoxical behaviour of the object*, which can always
be explained either by the subject's unworthy or clumsy behaviour which is only a ruse regarding his conviction, or by some
51 other cause such as shyness, the object's doubts, external influ-
ences acting on him, or a taste for putting the subject to the
test.

These *primary* ideas organize the entire delusion and will be discovered in all its developments. Whatever these developments possess that is vague and complicated relates only to secondary explanations relative to the obstacles encountered on the path to uniting the subject with the object. Behind this screen, one finds the robustness of the fundamental postulates, and even in the later stages of rancour and resentment, the following triad will persist:

- Pride,
- Desire,
- *Hope*.

To bring them to light, one must not so much question as manoeuvre the subject. One will thus bring out a forever enduring hope, a desire that is much less platonic than earlier authors have claimed, and an enduring pursuit.

PROGNOSIS AND DIAGNOSIS

The group of paranoiac psychoses is defined by their *intellectual integrity* independent of the delusion's specific structural disturbances.

Everything that tests can reveal about attention, memory and the necessarily broad tests of judgement and logical functions appears normal in these subjects.

The evolution, moreover, is *chronic with no dementia.*

Delusions in the paranoiac structure and delusions of inter- 52
pretation are *intractable* and will resurface outside the asylum despite the entirely superficial improvements, moreover generally based on dissimulation, that they may display.

On the contrary, they seem *soluble*, but in the most redoubtable way, in delusions of passion, which a criminal act extinguishes and assuages. This is true in general despite the odd cases of erotomanic delusion reoccurring on a second object, which were cited at the last forensic medicine conference.

One can see the importance of an accurate diagnosis. It is to be based on the positive signs we have been describing.

Very often, before turning to criminal acts, a delusional will have brought himself to the attention of the authorities through a series of complaints, written texts or threatening letters.

Pursuing internment measures here is very delicate and must be based essentially on the notion of delusion.

Writings are very valuable documents. They must be carefully collected, obtained at the time of entering the asylum, a time when the patient is in a favourably exalted sthenic state and has not yet learned to be reticent under the influence of his new environment.

Both types write very abundantly. The 'interpreters' are less rich regarding the particularities of handwriting – different sized letters, words underlined, arrangement of paragraphs – which, on the contrary, abound in the writings of the 'passionates'.[8]

53 Inquiries into social circumstances have to be thoroughly carried out.

We do not need to dwell on diagnosis regarding the large neighbouring groups: that of *paranoid psychosis*, on the one hand, which Henri Ey expands on here, and that of *external action syndromes*, on the other.

We have noted the very special *affective contact* of these psychorigid subjects. De Clérambault has noted that he is at variance with the welcome expansion of the chronically hallucinated, which finally explains his case.

A strict method is to be employed to explore the typical phenomena of mental automatism: act echoes, thought echoes and reading echoes; negative phenomena, etc.

Nor can we insist on a diagnosis with the allied *paraphrenias* and the *delusions of imagination*, which, related to our group by the absence of elementary logical disturbances, present different features:

- more decentred, more fanciful and with a certain aesthetic kind of unity in pure delusions of imagination;
- marked by themes of fantastical filiation, periodical return and repetition of the same events in certain paraphrenias;
- lastly, adopting, in other cases, an appearance of enormous egocentrism and absorption of the world into the ego, which gives them a quasi-metaphysical appearance.

[8] Thesis by S. Eliascheff, *Des écrits dans le délire d'interprétation* (Paris: Gisors, 1928).

This would be to revise the entire classification of delusions.

What I want to stress is the rigorous nature of these delusional types.

Any change in the delusion of interpretation type must 54
make us think of the acute interpretative states that may be symptomatic of mental confusion, the onset of general paralysis, sub-acute alcoholism, chronic hallucinatory psychosis, presenile involution, melancholia (with its delusion of self-accusation that is so different, centrifugal, resigned and bearing on the past), a so-called brief psychotic episode of the mentally retarded, or, lastly, a progressive paranoid dementia – each of these states having a quite different prognostic and therapeutic significance.[9]

Similarly, in delusions of passion and erotomania, any discordance in affective structure and any waning of sthenic reactions have to suggest a delusion symptomatic of dementia praecox, a cerebral tumour or an evolving syphilis.

FORENSIC REACTIONS AND INTERNMENT

These reactions, among the most frequent, present the most difficult problems to the alienist; they are at the base of social inadaptability and errors of judgement.

Chronic *rebellion* in the army. These are the type of inflexible rebels who end up being sent to a battalion in Africa once all disciplinary sanctions have been exhausted.

Scandal is what these subjects do – the anarchist's symbolic gesture or the conspiracy against the security of the State, which

[9] Thesis by Robert Valence, *Contribution à l'étude des états interprétatifs (en dehors du délire d'interprétation)*, Paris, 1927.

is doomed to failure, incidentally, because of their unbalanced ideas.

55 If the paranoiac, who is generally honest in his undertakings, is motivated to steal, he does so out of an altruism that is nothing other than a latent form of the hypertrophy of his ego, or out of a reasoned application of his social theories.

Propagandist, he struts around, all the way to the court house where he thinks more about the effect he will produce than about his fate. It can be an eminently contagious example.

The *murderous reaction* is the case that arises most often and is the axis of the whole problem for the alienist.

It stems either from the terrain itself, as with the vigilante killers, political assassins or mystical assassins who coldly plan their act over years and, once their act has been carried out, allow themselves to be arrested without resistance, declaring themselves satisfied with having taken the law into their own hands.

An already formed delusion of interpretation enters into play more often. This is a reaction that can be directed at any point of the network in which the subject's life is entangled. This subject is, in fact, an eminently dangerous one. Sometimes, it is only a matter of acts of violence or gestures as a warning to the persecutors.

Lastly, delusions of passion focus entirely on the act and carry it out efficaciously. It is often brought on by a paroxysm of emotion and anxiety. Consider the family crime of the murderous stepmother, etc.

Suicide reactions may occur in the 'interpretative' type.

Also note their distinctive *fugues* inspired by the curiosity that can sometimes give their delusion a special tone: for how long will they look for me?

Before the paranoiac gets to these reactions, he draws atten- 56
tion to himself through complaints to the police, letters to the Public Prosecutor and threats to individuals which make it possible to trace him but pose a very difficult problem for police and for medical intervention.

These delusionals and paranoiacs make up the majority of cases of 'arbitrary detention' that public opinion finds disturbing. They can excel as agitators.

The intellectual integrity, the relative [social] adaptation of these subjects and the decline of their troubles in the asylum, difficult to distinguish from their deliberate reticence, raise the most sensitive problems.

We can agree on the following principles:

Every *delusional* paranoiac must be detained.

In the asylum, his protests must be communicated regularly and without exception to the competent administrative authorities. However, he must be separated as much as possible from any person incapable of soundly judging the subject's psychological state.

When dealing with *criminal* acts, the expert must take into account the fact that these are subjects who are much more difficult to intimidate than others. Diminished responsibility therefore seems to be the worst approach.

Therefore, one must either let justice take its course or decide on detention, leaving it up to the patient to appeal to the tribunal.

Similarly, in the case of young *draft-dodgers* [*insoumis du service militaire*], there is an interest, in the face of the certain
failure of an increasing scale of disciplinary penalties, in direct- 57
ing these patients as early as possible to military justice, which in turn can refer them to a psychiatrist.

Regarding these subjects, we currently lack the means of appropriate social protection.

GENESIS AND PROPHYLAXIS OF THE PARANOIAC PSYCHOSES

The term 'paranoiac constitution' is justified by the early fixation of a structure. This fixation, which emerges clinically between early childhood and puberty, may be fully manifest as early as the age of seven and may occasionally become apparent only after the twentieth year.

It is to early childhood, and especially the early affective stages called the narcissistic or oral stages, that psychoanalysts trace the determining causes.

The influence exerted by the family environment, at the time of the appearance of the first reasoning concepts, has appeared to be no less important to attentive observers.

And according to the American school (Allen), careful social studies always reveal anomalies in the observed child's relations with the members of his family in the *home environment*: the influence of a stepmother or stepfather, bullying by or simply dominance of a brother or sister, hurtful emotional preferences or clumsy forms of punishment.

The emotional type of subject, especially the very isolated, emotionally inhibited type, which rests on neuro-vegetative bases, is said to be particularly favourable to the nascence of the [paranoiac] constitution.

58 A rather high rate of neurasthenic heredity (70%) among hospitalized paranoiacs (2% of patients – and mostly men, according to Kraepelin) has been reported. The difficulty of obtaining overall statistics for paranoiacs calls for caution. Note, here, the absence of any so-called classical somatic signs of degeneration in these states.

For delusions of interpretation, to what triggering causes are we to attribute their appearance on predisposed terrain? Sometimes, as I have said, one can identify an endogenous or exogenous toxic episode, an anxiety process, the outbreak of an infection, or an emotional trauma.

It is in the direction of the study of oneirism and oneiric states, along with the *post-oneiric remnants* of acute intoxication that one should, or so it seems to me, be looking for the grounds of a coherent mechanism of the onset of delusions.

Regarding the value of delusions themselves, do they represent one of these lower functions of the mind [*psychisme*] that are revealed when it is freed of control and of the higher inhibitions – a conception whose schema borrowed from neurology is tempting in its simplicity? Can they even be compared to certain forms of *primitive thought*, according to the phylogenetic conceptions of Tanzi and the Italians? This is a field in which nothing has come to test the hypotheses.

It is certain that delusions of passion, on the other hand, appear on the terrain of *neurasthenic heredity*. They are related to the categories of morbid impulsiveness and to the more or less revamped concept of degeneration. It seems that somatic *stigmata* are found much more frequently here.

The therapeutic difficulty is indicated well enough by the essentially chronic feature that forms part of the very description of these delusions.

Technicians of the unconscious, at the frontier of paranoia, 59
confess their inability to cure, if not to explain.

According to recent studies by Americans, it seems that a useful *prophylaxis* may be able to be usefully introduced *in childhood* by well-trained educators.

'Inspired' Writings: Schizography 61

PUBLISHED IN *ANNALES MÉDICO-PSYCHOLOGIQUES*, 1931*

Under the heading of 'schizophasia', a number of authors have emphasized the high value attached to certain more or less incoherent forms of language, not solely as symptoms of certain deep-seated disturbances of thought, but also as indicators of the stage of their evolution and their hidden mechanism.[1] In some cases, these disturbances only appear in written language. We will only attempt to show what material these writings offer to a precise study of psycho-pathological mechanisms. And this regarding a case that strikes us as unusual.

It concerns a patient, Marcelle C., 34 years of age, primary school teacher, hospitalized for a year at the psychiatric Clinic. She had been hospitalized for the first time a year and a half before, but had been released immediately at the request of her father, a modest tradesman.

Mlle C. initially gives the impression of a person who enjoys the full use of her faculties. Nothing unusual in her manner. No abnormal behaviour had been observed at any time in her life, in her employment. Very strong protest at her hospitalization

* Co-authors J. Lévy-Valensi, P. Migault and J. Lacan.

[1] Charles Pfersdorff, 'La Schizophasie; les catégories du langage', *Travaux de la clinique psychiatrique de Strasbourg* 5 (1927): 37–148; Guilhem Teulié, 'La Schizophasie', *Annales médico-psychologiques* 1 (February–March 1931): 113–23.

initially seemed to preclude any contact. It was nevertheless established.

62 Her remarks at that time were quite lively, focused, appropriate and sometimes cheerful. We undertook an objective examination, using a series of tests, of the integrity of her intellectual functions, which seemed complete in an extended conversation. As the ordinary tests regarding attention, logic and memory showed her as well below her capacities, we employed more subtle tests that were closer to the elements which our everyday evaluation of minds relies on. These are 'intention tests': the apparent and actual meaning of a statement, epigram, text, etc. She always showed herself to be competent, rapid and even confident.

Note that, however much one gains her trust, the affective contact remained incomplete. A deep-seated resistance is constantly asserting itself. At any given moment, moreover, the patient will declare, 'I do not wish to submit to anyone. I have never wanted to let myself be dominated by a man', etc.

When we reached the point at which this observation was made, the patient had fully externalized her delusion. It included a number of themes, some of which were typical:

- A theme of litigiousness [*revendication*], based on a series of failures at an examination that were held to be without justification, appeared in a series of actions pursued with sthenic passion and which provoked scandals that led to the patient's hospitalization. As damages for being hospitalized, she demands 'twenty million in compensation, of which twelve are for the deprivation of intellectual satisfactions and eight for the deprivation of sexual satisfaction'.
- A theme of hatred centred on one person, Mlle G., whom she accuses of stealing the place that was hers in the examination and taking her place in the position

she should have occupied. These aggressive feelings 63
extend to several men that she had met recently and for whom she appears to have quite ambivalent feelings – without ever having given into them, she affirms.

- An erotomanic theme with respect to one of her superiors in education, inspector R. – atypical in that it is retrospective, the object of the delusion being deceased and the morbid passion not having in any way revealed itself while he was alive.
- An 'idealistic' theme is externalized no less willingly. She has the 'sense of humanity's evolution'. She has a mission. She is a new Joan of Arc, but 'better educated and from a higher level of civilization'. She is made for guiding governments and regenerating morals. Her field is 'a centre linked to high international and military things'.

On what foundations does this polymorphous delusion rest? As we will see, this question remains problematic, and perhaps her writings will help us find the answer.

At the time of her two hospitalizations, the patient was examined in the Special Infirmary. The reports by Dr Logre and Dr de Clérambault emphasize the paranoiac nature, 'either old or recently formed', and acknowledge the presence of mental automatism.

While the paranoiac character appeared a long time ago in the patient, it was difficult to pinpoint when exactly, either by questioning, because of retrospective interpretations, or by making inquiries, since the only information we have had from the family has been by correspondence.

Nevertheless, merely reading the patient's *cursus vitae* seems to reveal a wish to differentiate herself from her family milieu,
a voluntary isolation from her professional milieu and errors of 64
judgement that become apparent in the facts. Her studies are

good, and there is nothing of note up till the time she finishes teacher training at 21 years of age. But, having gained a position in 1917, she believes she can acquit her duties in her own way, is already litigious and even interpretative. Several years later, she gets it into her head to become a teacher in a school of commerce, to this effect requests a change of position then a leave of absence and, in 1924, purely and simply resigns her position so as to prepare for her examinations in Paris. There, she earns a living employed as an accountant, but thinks she is being persecuted wherever she works and changes jobs twelve times in four years. The sexual behaviour we have alluded to and the deep-seated nature of the rebellion displayed by the patient, plus the impression that emerges from the entirety of her history, indicate an old, progressive anomaly of the personality of the paranoiac type.

Evaluating the 'imposed', or so-called external action elementary phenomena required a great deal of patience. In effect, it is not just the patient's reticence or trust that contributes to their dissimulation or disclosure. It is the fact that their intensity varies, that they develop in intermittent spikes, and that with these phenomena a state of effusive sthenia appears, which, on the one hand, doubtless gives them their convincing resonance for the subject and, on the other, renders them impossible to conceal, even for the purposes of defence.

During her stay in hospital, the patient displayed one such
65 spike, after which her avowals remained [*restés acquis*]: from this point she has informed us about the less intense and less frequent phenomena she experiences in intervening periods and on previous progressive episodes.

The phenomena of 'external action' come down to the subtlest that one could ever find in a morbid consciousness. At every moment of its evolution, our subject has always energetically denied ever having had 'voices'; she similarly denies any 'receptor [*prise*]', any echo of thoughts, of acts or of reading. When interviewed according to the indirect forms that experience with these patients has taught us to use, she says that she knows nothing about 'this scientific mumbo-jumbo that the doctors have tried to drag her into'.

At most, we are dealing with episodic hyperendophasia, nocturnal flight of ideas and psychical hallucinations. On one occasion, the patient hears the names of flowers at the same time as she smells their scent. On another, the patient sees and smells herself at one and the same time in a sort of internal vision, coupled with Inspector R. in a bizarre position.

Genital erethism is certain. The patient practices masturbation assiduously. It is accompanied by reveries, some of which are semi-oneiric. It is difficult to work out what part genital hallucination plays.

On the other hand, she experiences feelings of influence intensely and frequently. They are 'psychical affinities', 'intuitions', 'spiritual revelations' and feelings of 'direction'. 'There is a great subtlety of intelligence', she says. She distinguishes between the sources of these 'inspirations': Foch, Clemenceau, her grandfather, B. V., and above all her former inspector, M. R.

Lastly, we must classify the interpretations with the imposed givens of her pathological experience. At certain times, words and gestures in the street are meaningful. Everything has been
staged. The most banal details assume an expressive value 66
that concerns her destiny. These interpretations are currently active but unclear: 'I have come to understand that my case has become a parliamentary matter, . . . but it is so veiled, so unclear.'

Let us add some notes on the patient's somatic state. They are above all negative. The following must be retained: Influenza in 1918. Patent caffeinism. Irregular diet. Clear and persistent trembling of the fingers. Marked hypertrichosis of the lips. Regular periods. All other functions normal. Two very brief episodes of lipothymia when she was a teacher, with no organic sign other than a papillary cyst that lasted about a week. Tuberculosis common in the maternal line.

Let's now turn to her very abundant writings. We will publish a selection that is as integral as possible. We have inserted numbers to help refer back to the text in the commentaries that follow.[2]

I. Paris 30 April 1931

Mon cher papa, plus de quatre mois que je suis enfermée dans cet asile de Sainte-Anne sans que j'aie pu faire l'effort nécessaire pour te l'écrire. Ce n'est pas que j'aie quoi que ce soit de névralgique ou de tuberculeux, mais on t'a fait commettre l'an dernier de telles sottises mettant, en malhonnête, à profit ta parfaite ignorance de ma réelle situation (1) que j'ai subi le joug de la défense (2) par le mutisme. J'ai appris	My dear Dad, I have been locked up in this Sainte-Anne asylum for more than four months, unable to make the effort required to write to you. It is not that I have had anything neuralgic or tubercular, but last year they made you do such stupid things and, dishonestly, taking advantage of your perfect ignorance of my real situation (1) that I have undergone the yoke of defence (2) by remaining silent. I have nevertheless

[2] Owing to the unusual nature of her writings, we present the French original and the English translation in parallel. It has not on the whole been possible to render into English the spelling and grammatical idiosyncrasies of the original, nor more than a part of its semantic oddities. – Trans.

toutefois que le médecin de mon cas, à force de lenteur t'a mis en garde contre la chose grotesque et je vois qu'il a, sans plus soif d'avatars (3), mis les choses en parfaite voie de mieux éclairci (4) et de plus de santé d'État (5).	learned that the doctor for my case, by dint of his slowness has put you on your guard against the grotesque thing and I see that he has, without more thirst for avatars (3), placed things in a perfect pathway for better clarified (4) and for more State health (5).	
Daigne (6) intercepter les sons de la loi pour me faire le plus (7) propre de la terre sinon le plus (7) érudit. Le sans soin de ma foi (8) fait passer Méphisto (9) le plus (7) cruel des hommes mais il faut être sans doux dans les mollets pour être le plus prompt à la transformation. Mais il est digne d'envie qui fait le jeu de la manne du cirque. On voit que etc.	Deign (6) to intercept the sounds of the law to make me the cleanest (7) on earth if not the most (7) erudite. The care less of my faith (8) makes Mephisto (9) pass [for] the most (7) cruel of men but one must be without soft in the calves to be the readiest for the transformation. But he is worthy of envy who plays into the hands of the manna of the circus. One sees that etc.	67

II. Paris 14 May 1931

Monsieur le Président de la République P. Doumer en villégiaturant dans les	To the President of the Republic P. Doumer holidaying in

pains d'épices et les troubadoux,	gingerbread and the sweet minstrels,
Monsieur le Président de la République envahie de zèle,	Mr President of the Republic overcome with zeal,
Je voudrais tout savoir pour vous faire le (15) mais souris donc de poltron et de canon d'essai (16) mais je suis beaucoup trop long à deviner (17). Des méchancetés que l'on fait aux autres il convient de deviner que mes cinq oies de Vals (18) sont de la pouilladuire et que vous êtes le melon de Sainte vierge et de pardon d'essai (19). Mais il faut tout réduire de la nomenclature d'Auvergne car sans se laver les mains dans de l'eau de roche on fait pissaduire au lit sec (20) et madelaine est sans trader la putin de tous ces rasés de frais (21) pour être le mieux de ses oraies (22) dans la voix est douce et le teint frais. J'aurais voulu médire de la tougnate (23) sans faire le	I would like to know everything in order to make the (15) but mouse therefore of coward and of trial cannon (16) but I am much too long in guessing (17). Of the malicious things one does to others it is appropriate to guess that my five Vals geese (18) are of the flea-training and that you are the melon of the Holy Virgin and the trial pardon (19). But everything has to be reduced from the Auvergne nomenclature for without washing one's hands in rock water one does pisstraining in the dry bed (20) and madelaine is without trading the whore of all those freshly shaved (21) so as to be the best of her goldaries (22) whose voice is low and complexion

préjudice de vie plénière et de sans frais on fait de la police judiciaire (24). Mais il faut étonner le monde pour être le faquin maudit de barbenelle et de sans lit on fait de la tougnate (25).	fresh. I would have liked to maledict the bitch (23) without prejudicing the plenary life and at no cost one acts as the judiciary police (24). But one must astound the world in order to be the accursed knave of barbenelle and the bedless one acts like a bitch. (25)
Les barbes sales sont les fins érudits du royaume de l'emplâtre judice (26) mais il faut se taire pour érudir (27) la gnogne (28) et la faire couler sec dans si j'accuse je sais ce que j'ai fait (29).	The dirty beards are the fine erudites of the kingdom of the judice (26) dimwit but one has to be silent to erudire (27) the twit (28) and make him run dry in if I accuse I know what I have done. (29)
(31) À londoyer (30) sans meurs on fait de la bécasse (31) mais la trace de l'orgueil est le plus haut Benoit que l'on puisse couler d'ici longs faits et sans façon. Le péril d'une nation perverse est de cumuler tout sur le dos de quelqu'un et faire de l'emplâtre le plus maigre arlequin alors qu'il est préjudice à qui l'on veut,	(31) In baptising (30) without customs one acts like a silly goose (31) but the trace of the pride is the highest Benedict that one can flow from here long deeds and without a fuss. The peril of a perverse nation is to collect everything on someone's back and to make the dimwit the skinniest harlequin whereas he is harm to

	bonté à coups redoublés à qui l'on ne voulait pas pour soi.	whoever you like, goodness with redoubled blows on the one you wouldn't want for yourself.
68	Mais je vous suis d'accord pour le mot de la gloire du Sénat. Cureur (32) était de sa « c'est ma femme qui l'a fait » (33) le plus érudit de tous mais le moins emprunté.	But I agree with you for the word of the glory of the Senate. Secutor (32) was of his 'it was my wife that did it' (33) the most erudite of all but the least borrowed.
	À vous racler la couane je fais de la mais l'as est bonne il nous la faut bondir (34) mais je suis de ce paillasson qui fait prunelle aux cent quoi j'ai fait de l'artichaut avec ce fin bigorneau. Mais il faut passer brenat te fait le plus plein de commères, de compère on fait le ventre pour le faire suler de toi.	By scrubbing your hide I make molasses is good we have to make it leap (34) but I am from this doormat that makes liqueur to the hundred although I've made artichoke with this fine periwinkle. But one has to pass bran makes you the fullest of godmothers, of godfather one swells up to make him drunk with you.
	À moi d'avoir raclé la couane te fait la plus seule mais s'il est un tourteau c'est pour bonheur ailleurs et pas dans ces oraies-là elles sont trop basses.	By my having scrubbed the hide makes you the loneliest but if there is a crab it's for happiness elsewhere and not in those goldaries they are too low.

À vous éreinter je fais de l'âme est lasse (37) à toujours vous servir (35) et voir grimper les échelons à qui ne peut les gravir en temps et en heure. Il faut pour cela être gentille amie de l'oracle du Désir (36) et si vous êtes le feu de vendredettes (37) je vous fais le sale four de rat, de rat pâmé (38) et de chiffon de caprice.	By having exhausted you I make the soul is weary (37) to always serve you (35) and see climb the ranks to someone who cannot work his way up in time and in hour. For that one has to be the kind friend of the oracle of Desire (36) and if you are the fire of Frideedebts (37) I will make the dirty rat's oven for you, the fainted rat (38) and the rag of whim.
La tourte est le soin qu'on a pour l'adolescent quand il fait ses dents avec le jarret d'autrui (39). Son préjudice est celui qu'on n'éteint pas d'un coup d'ombrelle (40). Il faut le suivre à l'essai quand on l'a érudit (41) et si vous voulez le voir pâmer aller sans plus tarder avenue Champs-Élysées en si doré frisson (42) de la (80) patrouille des melons de courage mais de naufrage plein le jarret (44).	The pie is the care one has for the adolescent when he is cutting his teeth with the hock of others (39). His harm is the one that cannot be extinguished with a blow of a parasol (40). You have to follow him to the test when one has erudited him (41) and if you want to see him swoon go without delay to the avenue Champs-Élysées in such a gilded shiver (42) of the (80) patrol of the brave melons but of shipwreck full to the hocks. (44)

	À vos souhaits maître ma pâme (45) à vos jarrets (46) et ma désinvolture à vos oraies plus hautes (47).	God bless you master my swoon (45) to your hocks (46) and my nonchalance to your aforementioned orifices (47).
	Bastille Marcelle (48) autrement dit Charlotte la Sainte, mais sans plus de marmelade je vous fais le plus haut fiston de la pondeuse et de ses troupeaux d'amis verts pour me ravir le fruit de sentinelle et pas pervers. Je suis le beau comblons d'humour de sans pinelle et du Vautour, le peloton d'essai (49) et de la sale nuire pour se distinguer à tous rabais des autres qui veulent vous surpasser parce que meilleur à fuir qu'à rester.	Bastille Marcelle (48) otherwise known as Charlotte la Sainte, but without any more marmalade I make you the highest laddy of the egg-layer and her flocks of green friends so as to steal from me the fruit of sentinel and not perverse. I am the handsome one let's fill with humour without pinelle and Vulture, the test platoon (49) and the dirty to harm in order to distinguish oneself to all reductions from the others who want to surpass you because better to flee than stay.
69	Mes hommages volontaires à Monsieur Sa Majesté le Prince de l'Ironie française et si vous voulez en prendre un brin de cour faites le succès d'accord de	My voluntary respects to Mr His Majesty the Prince of French Irony and if you want to take a tad of courting make the success okay of Madelaine and of without

Madelaine et de sans tort on fait de l'artisan pour vous démoder, portefaix. Ma liberté, j'en supplie votre honnête personne, vaudra mieux que le barême du duce le mieux appauvri par parapluie d'escouade.	wrong one plays the craftsman so as to put you out of fashion, porter. My freedom, I beg of your honest person, will be worth more than the scale of the best impoverished Duce by a squad's umbrella.
Je vous honneurs, Monsieur Ventre vert (50). À vous mes saveurs de pétulance et de primeur pour vous honorer et vous plaire. Mercière du Bon Dieu pour vous arroser de honte ou vous hantir de succès solide et équilibré. Marais haute de poissons d'eaux douces. Bedouce.	I honour you, Mr Green Stomach (50). To you my flavours of petulance and first fruit in your honour and for your pleasure. Haberdasher of the Good Lord to spray you with shame or haunt you with solid and balanced success. High swamp of freshwater fish. Bedouce.

III. Paris, 4 June 1931

Monsieur le Méricain (51) de la buse et du prétoire,	Mr Merican (51) of the hawk and the praetorium,
S'il est des noms bien mus pour marquer poésie le somme des emmitouflés (52) oh ! dites, n'est-ce pas celui de la Calvée (53). Si	If there are well moved names to mark poetry the sum of the swaddled (52) oh! Tell me, isn't he the one from Calvée (53). If I had done

j'avais fait Pâques avant les Respans (54), c'est que mon École est de vous asséner des coups de butor tant que vous n'aurez pas assuré le service tout entier. Mais si vous voulez faire le merle à fouine (55) et le tant l'aire est belle qu'il la faut majorer de faits c'est que vous êtes as (58) de la fête et qu'il nous faut tous pleurer (56). Mais si vous voulez de ce lieu-ci sans i on fait de l'étrange affaire c'est que combat est mon souci et que, etc.	Easter before Palm Sunday (54), it's because my School is to beat you up with loutish blows as long as you have not provided the full service. But if you want to play the stickybeak blackbird (55) and the so beautiful is the area that one must augment it with facts it's that you are ace (58) of the feast and that we all have to cry (56). But if you want to have anything to do with this place without i one is making of the strange affair it's that combat is my worry and that, etc.

IV. Paris, 27 July 1931

Monsieur le Préfet de Musique de l'Amique (61) entraîné de style pour péristyliser le compte Potatos et Margoulin réunis sans suite à l'Orgueil, Breteuil.	Mr Prefect of Music of Amique (61), trained in style in order to peristylize the Potatos and Hustler account brought together without further action to Pride, Breteuil.
J'aime à voir conter le fait de l'Amérique en pleurs, mais il est si doux faits	I love to see told the fact of America in tears, but it is such sweet facts that one

qu'on fait longue la vie des autres et suave la sienne au point, qu'il est bien cent fois plus rempli celui qui vit de l'âcre et du faussaire et fait sa digne existence de la longue épître qu'il a cent fois sonné dans son gousset sans pouvoir de ce « et » faire un beau « maîtrisez-moi » (62) je suis cent fois plus lâche que pinbèche mais faites la fine école et vous êtes le soleil de l'Amérique en pleurs.	makes the life of others long and one's own suave to the point, that he is indeed one hundred times more full who lives on the acrid and the forger and makes his worthy existence from the long epistle that he has one hundred times rung in his gusset without being able with this 'et [and]' to make a fine 'master me' (62) I am one hundred times more cowardly than Madam Lah-di-dah but play the fine school and you are the sun of America in tears.
Mais à scinder le tard on fait de l'agrégée en toutes les matières et si matelotte est fait de boursiers et de bronzes à tout luire, il faut de ce « et Con ? » (63) faire un « salut à toi, piment tu nous rends la vie suve et, sans toi, j'étais pendant aux buttes de St-Clément. »	But in splitting the late one plays at being qualified in all subjects and if sailorette is made of scholarship holders and all-lustrous bronzes, one must with this 'and stupid?' (63) make a 'greetings to you, spicy you make our life su[a]ve and, without you, I and the bluffs of St. Clément were a pair.'
Le sort « tu vois ma femme, ce qu'on fait de la sorce »	The destiny 'you see my wife, what one makes

te fait le plus grand peintre de l'univers entier, et, si tu es de ceux qui font : poète aux abois ne répond plus, mais hélas ! il est mûr dans l'amur de l'autre monde, tu feras, je crois Jésus dans l'autre monde encore, pourvu qu'on inonde le pauvre de l'habit du moine qui l'a fait (64).	of the strength [or, possibly source]' makes you the greatest painter of the whole universe, and, if you are one of those who go: poet in dire straits no longer answers, but alas! he is ripe in the luv of the other world, you will do, I believe Jesus in the other world still, provided that one inundates the poor in the habit of the monk who made him (64).
Mon sort est de vous emmitoufler si vous êtes le benêt que je vois que vous fûtes, et, si ce coq à l'âne fut le poisson d'essai (65), c'est que j'ai cru, caduque que vous étiez mauvais (66).	My fate is to swaddle you if you are the simpleton that I see that you were, and, if this digression was the trial fish (65), it's that I believed, obsolete that you were bad (66).
Je suis le frère du mauvais rat qui t'enroue si tu fais le chemin de mère la fouine (67) et de sapin refait, mais, si tu es soleil et poète aux longs faits, je fais le Revu, de ce lieu-là j'en sortirai. J'avais mis ma casse dans ta bécasse. Lasse	I am the brother of the bad rat who makes you hoarse if you make mother's road the snoop (67) and from cop remade, but, if you are sun and poet of long facts, I make the Revu, from this place I will exit. I had put my breakages in your silly

de la tempête, j'achète votre tombe Monsieur (67).	goose. Tired of the tempest, I am buying your tomb, Sir. (67)
Marcelle Ch. aux abois ne répond pas aux poètes sans foi, mais est cent fois plus assassin que mille gredins.	Marcelle Ch. in dire straits does not answer faithless poets, but is a hundred times more of a murderer than a thousand scoundrels.
Genin.	Villain.

V. On 10 November the patient was asked to write a brief letter to the doctors in a normal style. She did it immediately, in our presence, successfully. She was then asked to write a post-script following her 'inspirations'. Here is what she gave us:

Post-Scriptum inspiré.	Inspired Postscript.	
Je voudrais vous savoir les plus inédits à la marmotte du singe (78) mais vous êtes atterrés parce que je vous hais au point que je vous voudrais tous sauvés (79). Foi d'Arme et de Marne pour vous encoquiner et vous faire pleurer le sort d'autres, le mien point (80).	I would like you to know you are the most unheard of to the marmot of the monkey (78) but you are appalled because I hate you to the point of wanting you all to be saved (79). Faith of Arm and Marne in order to hook up with you and make you cry over the fate of others, not mine at all (80).	71
Marne au diable.	Marne to the devil.	

Lastly, this letter, a true piece of 'poetic art', in which the patient describes her style.

VI. Paris, 10-12-1931

« Ce style que j'adresse aux autorités de passage, est le style qu'il faut pour bien former la besace de Mouléra et de son grade d'officier à gratter. »	'This style which I address to the interim authorities, is the necessary style to properly form Mouléra's bag and his officer rank to scrape.'
Il est ma défense d'Ordre et de Droit.	It is my defence of Order and Right
Il soutient le bien du Droit	It sustains the good of Right.
Il rigoureuse la tougne la plus sotte et il se dit conforme aux droits des peintres.	It rigorouses the stupidest bitch and says it conforms with the rights of painters.
Il cancre la sougne aux oraies de la splendeur, pour la piloter, en menin, dans le tougne qui la traverse.	It dunces the idiot in the orifices of splendour, to guide it, as a courtier, in the bitch who is passing through.
Il est Marne et ducat d' « et tort vous l'avez fait ? » (82)	It is Marne and ducat of 'and have you done wrong?' (82)

Ce m'est inspiré par le grade d'Eux en l'Assemblée maudite Genève et Cie.	This is inspired in me by the rank of Them in the accursed Assembly Geneva and Co.
Je le fais rapide et biscornu.	I do it quick and weird.
Il est final, le plus sage, en ce qu'il met tougne où ça doit être.	It is final, the wisest, in that it puts bitch where it has to be.
Bien-être d'effet à gratter.	Well-being of the effect for scraping.
Marcel le Crabe.	Marcel the Crab.

The handwriting is even from the letter's beginning to end. Extremely legible. Of the type called 'primary school'. Without personality but not without ostentation.

The end of the letter often fills the margins. Nothing else 72
original in the layout. No underlining.

Nothing has been crossed out. The act of writing, in our presence, is performed without pause and without haste.

The patient affirms that what she writes is imposed on her, not irresistibly nor even harshly, but in a way that is already formulated. It is 'inspired', in the strong sense of the term.

This 'inspiration' does not disturb her when she writes a letter in a normal style in the presence of a doctor. It arises, on the other hand, when the subject is writing alone and is always, at least periodically, welcome. Even in a copy of these letters meant for keeping, she does not dismiss a modification of the text that has been 'inspired' to her.

When asked about the meaning of her writings, the patient replies that they are easily understood. For recently composed writings, she mostly gives explanations that clarify the manner of their composition. We only take them into consideration subject to an objective analysis. With Pfersdorff, we only ever attribute the value of a symptom to so-called 'philological' interpretations.[3]

But in the main, the patient's attitude with respect to her writings, especially when they are old, breaks down into the following:

(a) Absolute conviction of their value. This conviction seems to be based on the sthenic state that accompanies her inspirations and brings about the conviction in the subject, even when incomprehensible to her, that they must express truths of a higher order. The idea that the inspirations are especially intended for the person to whom the letter is addressed appears
73 to be connected to this conviction. 'He will understand.' It is possible that the fact that she is pleading her case to the addressee (this is always the point of her writings) triggers the necessary sthenic state.

(b) Her perplexity over the meaning contained in her writings. This is where she claims that her inspirations are completely foreign to her and that she is in the same position regarding them as the interviewer. No matter how extreme this perplexity is sometimes, it leaves the initial conviction intact.

(c) As a justification, and perhaps decisive up to a point, she professes to being nonconformist. 'I am evolving language. All the old forms need shaking up.'

[3] Charles Pfersdorff, 'Contribution à l'étude des catégories du langage', *Travaux de la Clinique psychiatrique de la Faculté de Médecine de Strasbourg* 7 (1929): 307–57.

This attitude of the patient to her writings is identical to the structure of the entire delusion:

(a) Sthenic passion merging together the delusional feelings of hatred, love and pride in certainty. It correlates with states of influence, interpretation, etc.
(b) Formulation *a minima* of a delusion, as much litigious as erotomanic or reformist.
(c) Paranoiac background of overestimation of oneself and of errors of judgement.

This characteristic structure of delusion is displayed here in an exemplary manner.

Let us see if an analysis of the texts themselves sheds light on the internal mechanism of the phenomena of 'inspiration'.

Our analysis focuses on a collection of texts approximately ten times greater than the ones we have quoted.

To conduct this analysis without any preconceived ideas, 74
we follow the division of the functions of language that Head gives on the basis of purely clinical phenomena (the study of young aphasics).[4] Moreover, this conception fits remarkably well with what psychologists and philologists obtain with their own techniques.[5]

It is based on the organic integration of four functions to which correspond four types of disturbances effectively differentiated in a clinical setting: (a) verbal or formal disturbances to the written or spoken word; (b) nominal disturbances, or

[4] Henry Head, *Aphasia and Kindred Disorders of Speech*, 2 vols. (Cambridge: Cambridge University Press, 1926). Grouping these patients described as organic is not so bold as not to have been done already by several authors. See the report by Claude, Bourgeois and Masquin to the Société médico-psychologique of 21 May 1931.

[5] See Henri Delacroix, *Le Langage et la pensée* (Paris: Alcan, 1924).

disturbances of the meaning of words used, that is, of nomenclature; (c) grammatical disturbances, or disturbances of syntactic construction; (d) semantic disturbances, or disturbances of the overall organization of the meaning of a sentence.

A. VERBAL DISTURBANCES

Deterioration of word forms, indicative of a deterioration of the graphic motor schema, or of the auditory or visual image.

At first sight, the verbal disturbances are at a minimum. However, one encounters syllabic elisions (61), often bearing, remarkably, on the first syllable (26) (32) (51), quite frequently on the dropping of a particle [*et*, *ou*, *ni*, *mais*, *si*, *quand*, *que*, etc. in French], prepositions most often: '*pour* [for]', '*de* [of or
75 from]' or '*du* [of, from, some]' (9), etc. Are they brief impediments or inhibitions in the course of thought that form a part of the subtle negative phenomena of schizophrenia? It is all the more difficult to say, as the patient gives them delusional interpretations. She deletes this '*et*' or that '*de*' because it would have caused her task to fail. She alludes to this in her writings (62).

A number of verbal formulations, on the other hand, are clearly given by positive imposed elementary phenomena that are pseudo-hallucinatory (63); the patient often speculates on these phenomena.

The imposed character of certain phenomena is clearly apparent from the fact that their image is so purely auditory that the patient transcribes them in several different ways: '*la mais l'as*' (34), '*l'âme est lasse*' (37), also written as '*la mélasse*' in a poem that we have not cited. Likewise with '*le merle à fouine*' (55), '*la mère la fouine*' (67). The patient's denials, based on the difference in meaning, cannot overturn the fact, but on the contrary reinforce its validity.

One may thus wonder whether certain stereotypies that return insistently in one or several letters have a single origin: in Letter I, the '*d'État*' (5); in Letter II, the '*d'essai*' (16) (19) (49) [and in Letter IV] (65) that regularly attaches itself to words ending in '*on*', along the lines of '*ballon d'essai*', [and] in several letters, the '*si doré frisson*' (42) (60).[6] One may also ask oneself the same question for a whole series of stereotypies that appear in the text with a stamp of particularly poor absurdity, which, we would say, 'smell' of mental rumination and delusion. This is a distinction of an aesthetic order which, however, no one will fail to be struck by.

Yet, the neologisms appear to have a different origin in the 76
main, though some of them, like '*londrer, londoyer*' (31), resemble the sorts of neologisms produced by hallucinations. These are rare. For the majority, we have to classify them with nominal disturbances.

B. NOMINAL DISTURBANCES

Changes in the meaning of words seem to be similar to the processes of change studied by philologists and linguists in the way ordinary languages evolve. Like the latter, these changes occur through contiguity of the expressed idea, and also by contiguity of sound, or more exactly, the musical relatedness of words; false etymology of the popular kind sums up these two mechanisms: thus, the patient employs '*mièvre* [insipid, bland]' with the meaning of '*mesquin* [petty]'. She made a family out of '*mairie* [town hall]' and '*marier* [to marry]', from which she extracted '*mari* [husband]' and the neologism '*mairir*'.

The meaning is further transformed by way of the normal process of extension and abstraction, as in '*les jarrets* [hocks]'

[6] [The last reference is to a letter that has not been cited.]

– (39) (44) (46), etc. – frequently mentioned, a word to which she gives its literal meaning [back of the knee], and 'by extension' the meaning of struggle, march and active force.

Standard derivation processes produce neologisms: '*érudir* [to erudite]' (27) (41), '*énigmer* [to enigmate]'; '*oraie*' – (22) (47) – which formed [from '*or*', gold] like '*roseraie* [rose garden]', and very often used in the sense of business that produces gold; '*vendredettes*' (37), which designates whatever refers to a course she was taking on Fridays, etc.

77 Some of the other words have their origin in local or familial patois: see (28) and '*les Respans*' for '*les Rameaux* [Palm Sunday]' (54), the word '*nèche*' meaning wicked, nasty, naughty, and the words '*tougne* [bitch]', from which '*tougnate*' (23) (25) and '*tougnasse*' derive, and which are insults that always refer to her principal enemy, Mlle G. . .

Lastly, note the use of colourful language: '*les emmitouflés* [swaddled]', '*les encoquinés* [the hooked-up ones]', etc.

C. GRAMMATICAL DISTURBANCES

On examination one can see that syntactic construction is almost always respected. A formal logical analysis is always possible, provided one allows for the substitution of an entire sentence in place of a noun, as in the following example (56): '*Mais si vous voulez faire le merle à fouine et le / tant l'aire est belle qu'il la faut majorer de faits /. C'est que vous êtes as de la fête et qu'il nous faut tous pleurer.*' 'But if you want to play the sticky-beak blackbird and the / so beautiful is the area that one must augment it with facts /. It's that you are ace of the feast and that we all have to cry.' The two slashes separate off the sentence that plays the part of the noun. This construction occurs quite frequently (15) (24) (25) (29) (33) (73). Sometimes adjectives or adjectival forms are used as nouns: (4) (8) (17) (21), or simply a verb in the third person: '*le mena* [the lead]', '*le pela* [the pealed]', '*le mène rire* [the bring-to-laughter]'.

This form initially gives the illusion of a break in thought; as we see, it is the exact opposite, since the construction recommences after the sentence, which is in parentheses in a way, has been completed.

In some much rarer passages the syntactic link has been 78
destroyed and the terms form a verbal sequence organized by association by assonance of a manic type – (60) (73) – or by a discontinuous link of meaning, based on the last word in a group becoming the first word of the following group, a process akin to certain children's games: for instance (20); or, again, this passage: '*vitesse aux succès fous de douleur, mais ventre à terre et sans honneur*, speed towards mad successes of pain; but belly to the ground and without honour' (letter not cited). Fatigue is a factor in these forms, which are more frequent towards the end of letters.

D. SEMANTIC DISTURBANCES

These are characterized by what at first seems like total incoherence.

In reality it is pseudo-incoherence.

Some of the more accessible passages make it possible to recognize characteristic traits of thinking in which affectivity is predominant.

First, there is mainly ambivalence. 'I was subjected to the yoke of defence', she says, meaning precisely 'the yoke of oppression', for example. Even more clearly, 'You are appalled because I hate you to the point of wanting you all to be saved' (79). Cf. also (80).

Here are some examples of the condensation and agglutination of images. In an unpublished letter: '*Je vous serais fort*

avant-coureur de me libérer de cet enfer [I would be very forerunner for you to free me from this hell]', she writes to her local member of parliament. This means that in order to express her gratitude she will make him the beneficiary of these special insights that make her a forerunner of evolution. Similarly,
79 elsewhere: '*Je vous serais fort honnête de vouloir bien procéder à un emprisonnement correct dans l'enseignement primaire*, I would be very honest to you for wanting to proceed to a correct imprisonment in primary education.'

The displacement and projection of images are no less frequently observed after the patient has been interviewed. That she interprets (more or less secondarily matters little) an incoherent passage as expressing a lie about her that must have been going around, it turns out that words [*discours*] attribute the incriminating sentence to her. The inverse occurs just as frequently. The notion of participation seems here to efface that of the individual. And this tendency in her thought might stem from the delusional experience of the feeling of influence, were it not that the use of the procedure that we are flagging is clearly ironic and thereby reveals its affective dynamism.

There is further evidence of this in the profusion of proper names in her writings (several, one after the other, joined by an equals sign, =, to indicate the same individual, for example), the nicknames and the diversity and inventiveness of the names she signs off with.

Note that the patient frequently refers to herself in the masculine (7).

In a composition that we asked her to write on a technical topic it was assumed she would be familiar with, there was a very clear relation between the lack of direction and effectiveness of thought and this affective structure. This exercise, more or less adequate in its general content, two or three times showed her discourse going off track, completely off topic, and always in the form of irony, allusion and antiphrasis. These forms, in which affective thinking normally finds a way to express itself in a logical framework, was here linked to the manifestation of an intellectual deficit that had not been revealed by the tests in which she was passive.

Nevertheless, not everything in these texts seems to arise 80
from the degraded verbal formulation of affective tendencies. Apparent here is playful activity in which one must not misrecognize either the part played by intention or that played by automatism. Experiments carried out by a number of writers on a type of writing that has been called sur-realist, and whose method they have described very scientifically, show the remarkable degree of autonomy automatic writing can achieve even without hypnosis.[7]

Now, in these works, certain categories can be established in advance, such as an overall rhythm or a sententious form, without any reduction in the violently disparate character of the images that flow throughout.[8]

An analogous mechanism seems to play a role in the writings of our patient, where reading aloud reveals the essential role of rhythm. It can often carry considerable expressive power of its own.

The hexameter one finds on each line (66) is of little significance and is rather a sign of automatism. The rhythm can be given by a sententious construction which sometimes has the value of a true stereotypy, such as the schema given by the proverb: '*À vaincre sans péril on triomphe sans gloire* [Conquering without risk is to triumph without glory]', which underlies an apparently incoherent formula twenty times (31). A large

[7] André Breton, *Manifeste du surréalisme* (1924) [*Manifesto of Surrealism*, in his *Manifestoes of Surrealism* (Ann Arbor: University of Michigan Press, 1969)]; see André Breton and Paul Éluard, *L'Immaculée conception* (1930) [*The Immaculate Conception* (London: Serpent's Tail, 1992).]

[8] Paul Éluard and Benjamin Péret, *152 proverbes mis au goût du jour* (Paris: La Révolution Surréaliste, 1925); Robert Desnos, *Corps et Biens* (Paris: NRF, 1930).

number of turns of phrase specific to certain classical authors, La Fontaine very often, underpin the text. The most typical
81 of them is the delusional sentence just before the closing (53),
based on the famous couplet by Hégésippe Moreau:

S'il est un nom bien doux fait pour la poésie,
Ah: dites, n'est-ce pas celui de la Voulzie?
[If there is a sweet name made for poesy
Oh! Say, is it not that of Voulzie?]

In favour of such mechanisms of play, it is impossible not to note the remarkable poetic value that a number of passages attain, despite their faults. For example, the following two passages:

In Letter I, which we have only been able to give a part of, the following passages almost immediately follow our text:

On voit que le feu de l'art qu'on a dans les herbes de la St-Gloire met de l'Afrique aux lèvres de la belle emblasée.	One can see that the fire of the art one has in the grasses of St-Gloire puts some Africa on the lips of the beautiful emblaséd.

And still addressing her father:

Crois qu'à ton âge tu devrais être au retour de l'homme fort qui, sans civilisation, se fait le plus cran de l'aviron et te reposer sans tapinois dans le plus clair des métiers de l'homme qui	Believe that at your age you should be on the return from the strong man who, without civilization, makes himself the most notch of the oar and rest yourself without stealth in the

se voit tailler la perle qu'il a faite et se fait un repos de son amant de foin.	clearest of the trades of the man who sees himself cutting the pearl he has made and makes for himself a rest from his hay lover.

Also see (39) (40) (50) (64) (67).

At the conclusion of our analysis we can observe that it is impossible to isolate, in a morbid consciousness, any psycho-sensorial or purely psychical elementary phenomenon that would be a pathological nucleus to which an otherwise normal personality would react. Mental disturbances never occur in isolation. Here we see that the essential mechanism rests on a twofold foundation:

- an intellectual deficit which, as subtle as it is, finds 82
  expression in intellectual products and in behaviour, and is clearly the grounds of the delusional beliefs;
- a state of sthenic passion which, variously polarized into feelings of pride, hatred or desire, is uniquely rooted in an egocentric tendency.

This chronic emotional state is subject to variation according to several periods. Long periods, which exhibit a clinical correlation with the frequency of external action elementary phenomena. Short periods, which are brought on by the written expression of delusional themes.

In these exalted states, conceptual formulations, whether in the delusion or in the written texts, are no more important than the interchangeable lyrics of a song in couplets. Rather than the lyrics being the basis of the melody, the latter sustains the lyrics and justifies the fact that they are nonsense when the occasion arises.

This sthenic state is necessary for the phenomena we call 'elementary' – even if they possess psycho-sensorial consistency – to lead to delusional assent, which normal consciousness refuses to give.

Similarly, her writings only give the rhythmic formula, which has to be filled by the ideational contents as they present themselves. Given the state of the patient's intellectual level and culture, felicitous conjunctions of images will be produced every now and then, giving a highly expressive result. But most often, what comes out are the dregs of consciousness: words, syllables, obsessive sounds, 'refrains', assonances, various 'automatisms',
83 everything that a thought in a state of activity – that is, one that identifies reality – rejects and annuls with a value judgement.

Everything of this origin that is brought into the text is recognizable by a trait that signals its pathological character: stereotypy. This trait is sometimes apparent. Elsewhere, one can only sense it. For us, its presence is enough.

Nothing, in short, is less inspired, in the spiritual sense, than this writing experienced as inspired. It is when thought is brief and poor that the automatic phenomenon supplements it and is experienced as external because it is supplementing a deficit of thought [*déficit de la pensée*]. It is judged valuable because aroused by a sthenic emotion.

It seems to us that this conclusion, which touches on the most essential problems raised by the pathological functioning of thought, was worth the detailed phenomenological analysis that could only be possible with written texts.

The Problem of Style and the Psychiatric Conception of Paranoiac Forms of Experience 85

PUBLISHED IN 1933 IN THE FIRST ISSUE OF THE JOURNAL *LE MINOTAURE*

Of all the problems of artistic creation, I believe that style is the one that most urgently demands a theoretical solution, and, I believe, for the artist himself. Indeed, one not unimportant idea is that it is formed from the conflict, revealed through style, between a realist creation based on objective knowledge on the one hand, and on the other the superior force of signification or the high emotional communicability of what is known as stylized creation. According to this idea, in effect, the artist thinks of style as the result of a rational choice, an ethical choice, an arbitrary choice or even of an experience of a necessity whose spontaneity asserts itself against all control or, even, that one should release through a negative askesis. There is no need to stress the importance of these conceptions for theoreticians.

Now, it seems to me that the direction taken nowadays by research in psychiatry offers some new findings to these problems. I have shown the very concrete nature of these findings in detailed analyses applied to writings by the insane. I would like here to indicate in necessarily more abstract terms the theoretical revolution they bring to anthropology.

Academic psychology, as the most recent arrival of the posi- 86
tive sciences and thus appearing at the height of bourgeois civilization, which underpins the body of these sciences, could only pledge naïve confidence in the mechanistic thought that

had proven itself brilliantly in the physical sciences – at least, as long as the illusion of an infallible investigation of nature continued to conceal the reality of the manufacturing of a second nature more consistent with the mind's fundamental laws of equivalence, namely, that of the machine. Moreover, the historical progress of such a psychology, while it starts from the experimental critique of the hypostases of religious rationalism, ends, in the most recent psychophysics, in functional abstractions the reality of which is more and more rigorously reduced to a single measure – the physical output of human labour. Indeed, nothing in the artificial conditions of the laboratory could contradict such a systematic misrecognition of human reality.

It should have been the role of psychiatrists, which this reality solicits with a different urgency, to encounter both the effects of the ethical order in the transferences creative of desire or libido and the structural determinations of the noumenal order in the primary forms of lived experience: that is, to recognize the dynamic primordiality and originality of this experience (*Erlebnis*) in relation to every objectification of events (*Geschehnis*).

We would, however, be in the presence of the most surprising exception to the laws specific to the development of every ideological superstructure, had these facts been recognized as soon as encountered, affirmed as soon as recognized. The anthropology these facts imply renders the postulates of
87 rationalizing physics and morality too relative. But these postulates are sufficiently integrated into common language for the doctor – who, of all the different types of intellectuals, is the most constantly marked by a slight dialectical backwardness – not to have naïvely believed that he had found them in the facts themselves. Moreover, one must not fail to recognize that the interest in mental illness was historically born from needs that were juridical in origin. These needs appeared at the time

of the establishment, formulated as the basis of the law, of the bourgeois philosophical conception of man as endowed with absolute moral freedom and with responsibility intrinsic to the individual (link between the rights of man and the pioneering research of Pinel and Esquirol). Henceforth, the main question posed in practice to the science of psychiatrists has been the artificial question of all-or-nothing regarding mental decline [*déchéance*] (article 64 of the Penal Code).

It was therefore natural that at first psychiatrists would borrow their explanation of mental disorders from academic analyses and from the convenient schema of a quantitative deficit (deficiency or imbalance) in a function that relates to the world, where both function and world stem from the same abstraction and rationalization. An entire order of facts, one that corresponds to the clinical framework of forms of dementia, was, moreover, able to be fairly well resolved therewith.

It is a triumph of the intuitive genius specific to observation that Kraepelin, although entirely committed to these theoretical prejudices, was able to classify, with a rigour which has barely been added to, the clinical species the enigma of which, through often bastardized approximations (of which the public only retains the odd rallying word: schizophrenia, etc.), would
engender the unrivalled noumenal relativism of the viewpoints 88
of what is known as phenomenological contemporary psychiatry.

These clinical species are none other than the psychoses properly so-called (real 'madness', in the vernacular). Now, the work on these mental states inspired by phenomenology (for example, the most recent by Ludwig Binswanger on the state known as 'flight of ideas' observed in manic-depressive psychosis, or my own work on *La Psychose paranoïaque dans ses rapports avec la personnalité* [*Paranoiac Psychosis in its Relations with Personality*]) does not detach the local reaction – which is mostly noticeable because of pragmatic discrepancy [in behaviour], which can be individualized as a mental disturbance – from the patient's total lived experience, the specificity of which it is attempting to define. This experience can only be understood as being at the extremes of an effort to find agreement; it can be validly described as a coherent structure of an immediate noumenal apprehension of oneself and the world. Only a highly rigorous analytic method can make such a description possible; in fact, all objectification is eminently precarious in a phenomenal order that emerges prior to rationalizing objectification. The forms of these structures that have been explored make it possible to conceive of them as differentiated from one another by a number of hiatuses that make it possible to classify them.

Now, a number of these forms of lived experience, called 'morbid', present as especially rich in their symbolic modes of expression, which, although fundamentally irrational, nevertheless carry an eminent intentional signification and very high-tension communicability. They are found in the psychoses
89 that I have particularly studied, preserving their former – and etymologically satisfactory – label of 'paranoia'.

These psychoses manifest clinically as a delusion of persecution, a specific chronic progression and characteristic criminal reactions. Being unable to discern any problems in handling the logical apparatus and spatio-temporo-causal symbols, authors of a classical orientation have not been afraid to refer, paradoxically, all such problems to a hypertrophy of the reasoning function.

For my part, I have been able to show not only that the world specific to these subjects has been transformed much more in its perception than in its interpretation, but that this very perception is not comparable to the intuition of objects specific to the average civilized person. Indeed, on the one hand, the field of perception for these subjects is stamped with an immanent and imminent character of 'personal signification' (a symptom called 'interpretation'), and this characteristic excludes the affective neutrality of the object that rational knowledge requires, at least in principle. On the other hand, the decline, striking in these cases, in spatiotemporal intuitions modifies the impact of the conviction of reality (illusions of memory, delusional beliefs).

These fundamental features of the paranoiac lived experience exclude it from ethico-rational deliberation and from any phenomenologically definable freedom in imaginative creation.

Now, we have methodically studied the symbolic expressions of their experience as given by these subjects: they are, on the one hand, the ideational themes and significant acts of their delusion and, on the other hand, the plastic and poetic productions at which they are very prolific.

I have been able to show: 90

The eminently human signification of these symbols, whose only analogue regarding the delusional themes lies in the mythical creations of folklore, and, regarding the feelings nourishing their fantasies, is often not unequal to the aspirations of the greatest artists (feelings for nature, idyllic and utopian feelings regarding humankind and feelings of antisocial demands).

I have described a fundamental tendency in the symbols, which I have referred to by the term 'iterative identification of the object': the delusion shows itself to be very fertile, in fact, in fantasies of cyclical repetition, ubiquitous multiplication, endless periodic returns of the same events and doublets and triplets of the same people, sometimes in hallucinations duplicating the subject's person. These intuitions are manifestly related to the very constant processes of poetic creation and seem to be one of the conditions of typification, which creates style.

But the most remarkable point that we have extracted from the symbols engendered by psychosis is that their reality-value is in no way diminished by their origin, which excludes them from the mental community of reason. Delusions do not, in fact, need to be interpreted for them to express, by means of their themes alone, and wonderfully so, the instinctual and social complexes that psychoanalysis finds so very difficult to bring to light in neurotics. It is no less remarkable that the murderous reactions of these patients very frequently occur at a pressure point of social tensions at an historical moment [*actualité historique*].

All these features specific to paranoiac lived experience leave
91 it a margin of human communicability where, in other civilizations, it has demonstrated its full power. All the same, this has not been lost in our own rationalizing civilization: one can affirm that the fascination that the person and style of Rousseau, of whom the diagnosis of typical paranoia can be made with the highest degree of certainty, held over his century was due to his properly morbid experience. We can also see that the criminal act of paranoiacs can sometimes move our tragic sympathy to such an extent that this century, in order to defend itself, no longer knows whether to strip it of its human value or crush the guilty one under the weight of his responsibility.

One can think of the paranoiac lived experience and the conception of the world it engenders as an original syntax, one that contributes to an affirmation of the human community through its own specific bonds of understanding. Knowledge of this syntax seems to me to be an indispensable introduction to an understanding of the symbolic values of art and, in particular, the problems of style – specifically, of the virtues of conviction and human communion that are specific to it, no less than to the paradoxes of its origins – problems forever insoluble for any anthropology that has not been liberated from a naïve realism of objects.

Motives of Paranoiac Crime: the Papin Sisters' Crime 93

PUBLISHED IN *LE MINOTAURE*, NUMBERS 3/4, 1933

To Dr Georges Dumas, in respectful friendship

We all remember the horrible circumstances surrounding the massacre in Le Mans and the emotions aroused by the mystery regarding the motives of the two murderers, sisters Christine and Léa Papin. The concern and interest gave rise to a very full account of the facts, in the press, by the newspaper of the best-informed journalistic minds.[1] Consequently, I will only summarize the facts of the crime.

For several years, the two sisters, [Christine] 28 and [Léa] 21 years of age, had been servants in a respectable bourgeois family of a solicitor, his wife and daughter in this small provincial city. Model servants, it was said, envied for their housekeeping; mystery-servants also, for, while it had been observed that their masters oddly seemed to lack any human sympathy, there is nothing to suggest that the haughty indifference of the maids was anything more than a response to this attitude: 'We didn't speak to each other'. This silence could not have been empty, however, even if to the eyes of the participants it remained obscure.

[1] Cf. the articles by Jérôme and Jean Tharaud in *Paris-Soir*, 28, 29 and 30 September and 8 October 1933.

94 One evening, 2 February [1933], this obscurity materialized due to a banal outage of the electric lighting. It was caused by a blunder on the part of the sisters, and their absent employers had already displayed a lively reaction to more trifling matters. What was the mother and daughter's reaction on discovering this minor disaster on their return? Christine's words varied on this point. Be that as it may, the drama was very quickly triggered, and it is difficult to admit any other version of the form of the attack than the one given by the sisters, namely, that it was sudden, simultaneous and from the outset carried to a paroxysm of fury. They each grabbed an adversary, ripped their eyes from their sockets (something unheard of, it was said, in the annals of crime) and knocked them unconscious. Then, with the assistance of whatever lay to hand – hammer, metal jug, kitchen knife – they smashed in their faces and, exposing their genitals, made deep slashes into the thighs and buttocks of one and soiled the thighs and buttocks of the other with the blood. They then washed the instruments of these appalling rituals, cleansed themselves and lay down together in the same bed. 'A nice piece of work!' were the words they exchanged and they seemed to set the more sober tone, devoid of any emotion, that succeeded their orgy of bloodletting.

They gave the court no comprehensible motive for their act, no hatred, and no grievance against their victims; their sole concern seemed to be to totally share responsibility for their crime. To the three medical experts they appeared to lack any sign of delusion or dementia and any actual psychical or physical disorder – which is what they felt compelled to report.

95 The details of their history were too imprecise, it seems, for it to have been possible to take them into account: a confused approach by the sisters to the mayor to obtain the younger one's [legal] emancipation; a general secretary [of the prefecture] who thought they were 'crazy'; a superintendent of police who took them to be 'persecuted'. There is also the unusual attachment

that bound them to one another, their immunity to all other interests and their days off that they would spend together in their room. But were any of these strange goings-on cause for concern? I have omitted an alcoholic, brutal father who, it is said, raped one of his daughters and the early abandonment of their education.

It was only after five months in prison that Christine, separated from her sister, underwent a crisis in which she became extremely agitated, with terrifying hallucinations. Over the course of another crisis, she attempted to tear out her own eyes, unsuccessfully, but not without injuring herself. Her state of agitation this time required the use of a straitjacket. She engaged in acts of erotic exhibitionism, then melancholic symptoms appeared: depression, refusal to eat, self-accusations and expiatory acts of a repugnant kind. On several subsequent occasions, she engaged in speech with delusional meaning. I would say that Christine's declaration that she simulated some of these states can in no way be taken to hold the true key to their nature: a sense of play was frequently experienced by the subject, without her behaviour being any less typically morbid.

On 30 September, the sisters were found guilty by the jury. Christine, hearing that she would be beheaded in the square of Le Mans, received the news on her knees.

However, the nature of the crime, Christine's disturbed 96
behaviour while in prison and the oddness of the life of these sisters had convinced a majority of psychiatrists that the murderers were not responsible for their actions.

Faced with the refusal for a second opinion, Dr Logre, known to be a highly qualified specialist, took it upon himself to testify in court in their defence. Was it the principle of rigour inherent in this expert clinician or the care that the circumstances called for that placed him in the position of advocate? Dr Logre submitted not one but several hypotheses concerning the presumed mental anomaly of the sisters: ideas of persecution, sexual perversion, epilepsy or hystero-epilepsy. While I consider it possible to formulate a more univocal solution to the problem, I would first like to pay homage to his authority, not only because it shields me from the reproach of making a diagnosis without having examined the patients myself, but because, in its particularly well-chosen formulas, it endorses certain facts that are quite difficult to isolate, and yet, as we shall see, essential to the demonstration of my thesis.

There is a morbid entity, paranoia, which, despite the various fortunes it has undergone with the evolution of psychiatry, corresponds roughly to the following classical features: (a) an intellectual delusion whose themes range from ideas of grandeur to ideas of persecution; (b) aggressive and, very frequently, murderous reactions; and (c) a chronic progression.

Two conceptions of the structure of this psychosis have until now stood in opposition to one another: one takes it to be the development of a morbid 'constitution', that is, a congenital character flaw; the other points to its elementary phenomena in
97 momentary disturbances of perception, which are described as 'interpretative' because of their apparent analogy with normal interpretation. A delusion is here considered to be a rational effort on the part of the subject to explain these experiences, and the criminal act as a passionate reaction whose motives are given by the delusional conviction.

Although the existence of elementary phenomena is much more certain than the alleged paranoiac constitution, one can easily see the inadequacy of both conceptions, and I have attempted to establish a new conception on the basis of an observation that is more consistent with the patient's behaviour.[2]

[2] *De la psychose paranoïaque dans ses rapports avec la personnalité* (Paris: Le François, 1932). [Second edition, *De la psychose paranoïaque dans ses rapports avec la personnalité suivi de premiers écrits sur la paranoïa* (Paris: Seuil, 1975).]

In the elements of a delusion, in the delusion as a whole and in its reactions, I recognized the primordial influence of social relations incidental to each of these three orders of phenomena. And I introduced as explanatory of the facts of psychosis the dynamic notion of 'social tensions', whose state of either equilibrium or rupture normally defines the individual's personality.

The aggressive drive, which can result in murder, thus appears as the affliction that is at the basis of psychosis. It can be said to be unconscious, which means that the intentional content by which it is translated into consciousness cannot appear without compromise with the social demands integrated by the subject, that is, without camouflaging the motives, which is precisely the entire delusion.

But this drive is itself stamped with social relativity. It always has the intentionality of a crime, almost always that of vengeance, frequently the sense of punishment, that is, of a sanction arising from social ideals, and, lastly, it sometimes 98
identifies with a completed act of morality and has the significance of expiation (self-punishment). The objective features of murder, its choice of victim, its murderous effectiveness and ways of being triggered and executed vary in a manner that is continuous with these degrees of human signification of the fundamental drive. These same degrees drive society's reaction with respect to paranoiac crimes, an ambivalent reaction with a dual aspect that produces emotional contagion of the crime and [public] opinion's demand for punishment.

Such is the case of the Papin sisters' crime, in the emotion that it provokes – which goes beyond horror – through its value as an atrocious image, symbolic right down to its most hideous details: the most well-worn of metaphors: 'I'll tear his eyes out!' receives its literal execution. Popular consciousness reveals the meaning it gives this hatred by applying here the ultimate penalty, like ancient law regarding the crimes of slaves.

Perhaps, as we will see, it is mistaken about the real meaning of this act. But let's observe, for the use of those frightened by the psychological course on which we are embarking for the study of responsibility, that the adage 'to understand is to forgive' is subject to the limits of each human community and that, outside these limits, to understand (or to think one understands) is to condemn.

The intellectual content of a delusion seems to me, as I have already said, to be a superstructure that is both justificatory and negatory of the criminal drive. I think of it, then, as subject to the variations of this drive, to the collapse [*chute*] that, for example, results from its fulfilment. In the first case of the particular type of paranoia described by me (the case of Aimée), the delusion disappeared with the achievement of the act's aim.
99 I am not surprised that the same thing happened during the first months following the sisters' crime. The consequent deficiencies of the classical descriptions and explanations have for a long time led people to misunderstand the existence, which is nevertheless crucial, of such variations by affirming the stability of paranoiac delusions, whereas the only constancy is structural: this conception leads the experts to draw erroneous conclusions and explains their difficulties in the face of numerous paranoiac crimes, where their sense of reality surfaces despite their theories, but only engenders uncertainty in them.

In the case of the Papin sisters, we need only hold onto one single trace of the formulation of delusional ideas prior to the crime for a complement to the clinical picture. We know it can be found primarily in the testimony of the city's superintendent of police. His lack of precision can in no way lead to its rejection; every psychiatrist is aware of the very special atmosphere the patient's stereotypical words evoke, whatever their form, even before they become explicit in delusional formulas. Even if someone were to experience this impression just the once, the fact that he recognizes it cannot be considered negligible.

And one gets used to this experience in the triage functions in police stations.

Christine expresses several delusional themes in prison. I use this term to describe not only typical symptoms of delusions, such as the systematic misrecognition of reality (Christine asked how her two victims were and declared that she thought that they had returned in another body), but also the more ambiguous beliefs that translate into statements such as the following: 'I believe that in another life I would have been the husband of my sister.' It is, effectively, possible to recognize in these words the quite typical content of classified delusions. 100
Moreover, it is a constant to encounter a certain ambivalence in all delusional beliefs, from the most quietly affirmative forms of fantastical delusions (in which the subject nevertheless recognizes a 'double reality'), to interrogative forms of delusions, called 'delusions of supposition', in which every affirmation of reality is suspect for the subject.

In the present case, analysis of these contents and forms would enable us to specify the place of the two sisters in the natural classification of delusions. They would not fall under this very limited form of paranoia that I isolated in my work by employing formal correlations such as these. They would even lie outside the generic framework of paranoia and be included in the paraphrenias, which the genius of Kraepelin isolated as immediately contiguous forms. This clarification of the diagnosis would, however, be very uncertain given the chaotic state of our information. Moreover, it would be of little use to my study of the motives of the crime, since, as indicated in my work, the forms of paranoia and the neighbouring delusional forms remain unified by a structural affinity that justifies using the same methods of analysis.

What is certain is that the forms of psychosis in the two sisters are, if not identical, then at least closely correlated. Over the course of the debates, we have heard the astonishing claim

that it is impossible for two beings to be struck by the same madness together, or rather to exhibit it simultaneously. This claim is completely false. *Délire-à-deux* is amongst the oldest recognized forms of psychosis. Observations show that it tends to occur between members of the same family, father and son, mother and daughter, and brothers or sisters. Let's say that in
101 certain cases the mechanism arises from contingent suggestion exercised by an active, delusional subject on a passive, weak-minded subject. We shall see that my conception of paranoia gives quite a different account and explains in a more satisfactory way the parallel criminal action of the two sisters.

The murderous drive that I think of as the foundation of paranoia would be nothing but an unsatisfactory abstraction, were it not for the fact that it happens to be regulated by a series of anomalies correlated with socialized instincts, and that the current state of our knowledge about the development [*évolution*] of personality enables the genesis of these drive anomalies to be regarded as contemporaneous. Homosexuality and sado-masochistic perversion are the instinctual disturbances whose existence psychoanalysts alone have known, in this case, how to detect and whose developmental signification I have tried to show in my work. It has to be admitted that the sisters appeared to give what could be called a crude confirmation of these correlations: sadism is obvious in the acts perpetrated on the victims. And what signification cannot be found, in the light of these facts, in the exclusive affection of the two sisters for one another, the mystery of their life, the oddness of their cohabitation and their fearful clinging to one another in a single bed after the crime?

Our specific experience of these patients gives us pause, however, before asserting, as some people have, the reality of sexual relations between the sisters. This is why I am indebted to Dr Logre for the subtlety of the term 'psychological couple', in which one can evaluate his reticence concerning this problem.

Psychoanalysts themselves, when they derive paranoia from homosexuality, describe this homosexuality as unconscious, as 'latent'. This homosexual tendency is said to express itself only in a desperate negation of itself, which then grounds the 102
conviction of being persecuted and makes the loved one into a persecutor. But what is this unique tendency which, so close in this way to its most obvious revelation, would always remain separated from it by a uniquely transparent obstacle?

In an admirable article, Freud, without giving the key to this paradox, provides all the elements needed to find it.[3] He effectively shows that, when the forced reduction of primitive hostility between brothers comes into operation during the now-recognized first stages of infantile sexuality, an abnormal inversion of this hostility into desire may occur, and that this mechanism engenders a special type of homosexual in whom social instincts and activities predominate. As a matter of fact, this mechanism is a constant one: erotic fixation is the primordial condition for the first integration of what I call 'social tensions' into instinctual tendencies. It is a painful integration, in which the first sacrificial demands that society will never stop making of its members are marked: this is its link with the personal intentionality for inflicting suffering that constitutes sadism. This integration occurs, however, according to the law of least resistance through an affective fixation that is still very close to the solipsistic ego, a fixation that deserves to be called narcissistic and in which the chosen object is most like the subject: this is the reason for its homosexual character. But it is necessary to go beyond this fixation in order to arrive at a socially effective morality. Piaget's fine studies have shown the progress that takes place from the naïve *egocentrism* of the early

[3] Sigmund Freud, 'De quelques mécanismes névrotiques dans la jalousie, la paranoïa et l'homosexualité', trans. J. Lacan, *Revue Française de Psychanalyse* no. 3 (1932): 391–401. ['Some Neurotic Mechanisms in Jealousy, Paranoia and Homosexuality' (1922), *Standard Edition* 18: 223–32.]

103 participation in the rules of the moral game to the cooperative objectivity of an ideally complete [*achevée*] conscience.

In our patients this development did not go beyond the first stage, and the causes of such an arrested development can be of quite different origins, either organic ('hereditary defects') or psychological: psychoanalysis has revealed the significance of incest with children among the latter. We know that this act seems not to have been absent from the sisters' lives.

In fact, well before I made these theoretical comparisons, the lengthy observation of multiple cases of paranoia, supplemented by meticulous social inquiries, led me to the view that the structure of the paranoias and related delusions is entirely dominated by the outcome of this sibling complex. The main example of this among the observations I have published is striking. Affective ambivalence towards the older sister drove the entire self-punishing behaviour of our 'case of Aimée'. If Aimée successively transferred the accusations of her love–hate from one person to another over the course of her delusion, it was in an attempt to free herself of her first fixation; but the effort was abortive. Each of the women who persecuted her was really nothing other than a new image, always entirely a prisoner of narcissism, of this sister whom our patient had made into her ideal. We now understand what the invisible obstacle was that means she will never know, even though she was shouting it, that she loved all of these persecutory women – [namely,] that they are merely images.

The 'malady of being two' that these patients suffer from scarcely liberates them from the malady of Narcissus. A mortal passion, which ends by one's taking one's life. Aimée struck the glittering being she hated precisely because it represented
104 the ideal she had of herself. This need for self-punishment, this enormous sense of guilt, can also be read in the actions of the Papins, even if only in the act of Christine's kneeling at the end. But it seems that the sisters could not even assume the distance

from one another necessary for them to murder one another. True Siamese souls, they formed a world forever closed; reading their statements following the crime, Dr Logre said, 'It's like I'm reading in duplicate.' They had to resolve their enigma, the human enigma of sex, with their islet as their only means.

One needs to have listened with an attentive ear to the strange declarations of such patients to know what forms of madness their shackled consciousness is capable of devising around the enigmas of the phallus and feminine castration. Then one will know how to recognize, in the timid avowals of the so-called normal subject, the beliefs he keeps quiet, and which he believes he is keeping quiet because he judges them childish, whereas he keeps quiet because without knowing it he still holds them.

Christine's words, 'I believe that in another life I would have been the husband of my sister', are reproduced in our patients in many fantastical themes which, to obtain, one only has to listen. Down what long and tortuous path was she obliged to travel before the despairing experience of the crime ripped her from her other self and before she was able – following her first crisis of hallucinatory delusion in which she thought she saw her sister dead, dead no doubt from this blow – to cry out before the judge confronting them, the words of open-eyed passion, 'Yes, say yes!'?

That fateful night, in the anxiety of their imminent punishment, the sisters mingled the mirage of their malady with the image of their mistresses. It was their own distress that they detested in the couple whom they brought into a dreadful quadrille. They tore out their eyes just as the Bacchae castrated [their victims]. It was the sacrilegious curiosity that has formed man's anxiety from the depths of ages that fuelled them 105
when they tore their victims apart, when in their victims' open wounds they searched for what in her innocence Christine would later, before the judge, call 'the mystery of life'.

Psychology and Aesthetics 107

REVIEW OF E. MINKOWSKI, *LE TEMPS VÉCU*, PUBLISHED IN *RECHERCHES PHILOSOPHIQUES*, 1936

E. Minkowski. *Le Temps vécu. Études phénoménologiques et psychopathologiques.* 1 vol., 400 pages, collection 'Évolution psychiatrique', J. L. L. d'Artrey, Administrator, 17, rue de la Rochefoucauld, Paris.[1]

An ambitious and ambiguous work – so this reader judges it on turning the final page. The ambiguity, already apparent in the work's bipartite structure, reveals itself more profoundly in the double meaning of each of the two parts: a first 'essay' on 'the temporal aspect of life', whose phenomenological framework does not adequately justify the metaphysical postulates proclaimed within it; a second essay on the structure of mental disorders, focused on their spatiotemporal structure, the analyses of which, valuable for clinical work, owe their acuity to the coercion exerted on the observer by the object initially set up by his spiritual meditation.

These underlying contradictions would be tantamount to failure, were it not for the fact that the high standard of the work is assurance that it is only the failure inherent in its ambition, I mean failure linked to the phenomenology of this

[1] [Published in English as *Lived Time*, trans. Nancy Metzel (Evanston, Ill.: Northwestern University Press, 2019). All page references below are to the English edition.]

passion, to its structure which, for me, is packed with enigmas. Once this structure has been revealed, shall we look for its method in the authentic confidences by which the work betrays the personality of its author? I will mention one such
108 confidence (153), regarding Mignard's last work, 'a synthesis of his scientific and spiritual life – a synthesis so rare in our times, when we are in the habit of erecting an insurmountable barrier between the assumed objectivity of science and the spiritual needs of our soul' (153).

I want to start my critique with this and claim the right to restore the aforesaid barrier which, to be sure, is for me not insurmountable, but constitutes the sign of a new alliance between man and reality. I will, then, examine the threefold contents of the work in order: scientific objectification, phenomenological analysis and personal testimony, the movement of my analysis shall provide a synthesis of the work, should one exist.

The scientific contribution relates to the givens [*données*] of mental pathology. We know how imperfect objectification of it still is. One finds here valuable contributions to its development; they are all the more valuable for the fact that in the current state of the psychiatric literature in France a work such as this is exceptional. Nothing in all the communications that are made in official scientific societies offers anything other, in effect, than the image of the most miserable intellectual stagnation to anyone whose profession has had to make do with such disheartening information for what has already been so many years.

One takes as a valid scientific activity the simple juxtaposition, in a 'case', of a fact of psychopathological observation and a symptom that is generally somatic and classifiable in the category of so-called organic signs. One can adequately appreciate the exact significance of this work when one observes the kind of observations one is satisfied with here. The inanity of it
109 is guaranteed by the terminology that observers find adequate

for reporting it. This terminology comes entirely from faculty psychology, which, stuck in the academism of Cousin, has not been reduced by associationist atomism in any of its eternally scholastic abstractions: hence, this verbiage about images, sensations and hallucinations; about judgement, interpretation, intelligence, etc.; and, lastly, about affectivity, the latest arrival, the cliché in one moment of progressive psychiatry, which has found there the most appropriate term for numerous evasions. Regarding so-called organic symptoms, in standard medical practice, it is they that appear endowed with an importance entirely relative to the whole semiological procession; that is, rarely pathognomonic, they are more often probabilistic to a greater or lesser extent. In one particular form of psychiatry, on the other hand, they assume the value of a taboo which turns their mere discovery into a doctrinal conquest. Each discovery of this kind is taken to be another step in the effort to 'reduce psychiatry to the framework of general medicine'. The result of this ritual activity is that this method, that is, the mental apparatus without which the reality of a fact may be misunderstood, even when present, would still be a point in its favour in psychiatry, for sure – though one that it was possible to go beyond, as Falret, Moreau de Tours and Delasiauve had done – were it not for the work of rare researchers such as Pierre Janet, who happen to be so familiar with the implicit philosophy that paralyses the psychology of doctors that they were able to overcome it and extract themselves from its terms. Hence, the philosophical training whose role, time and earlier fruits M. Minkowski is careful to place in his own biography helped him greatly to appreciate the real nature of the facts with which 110
daily clinical experience subsequently provided him.

The novelty of method in Dr Minkowski's insights is their reference to the point of view of structure, a sufficiently foreign point of view, it seems, to the ideas of French psychiatry for many still to think that we are dealing with something equivalent to faculty psychology. Structural facts become known to the observer in the formal coherence that is displayed by different types of morbid consciousness, which combines, in a different way in each, the forms captured therein of the identification of the ego, of the person and of the object – of the intentionalization of the shocks of reality – and of logical, causal, spatial and temporal assertions. It's not at all a question of taking down the subject's declarations, which we have known for a long time (this is perhaps one of the points of psychiatric psychology that are now accepted) cannot fail but to be inadequate, because of the very nature of language, to the lived experience the subject attempts to express. It is, rather, despite language, a question of 'penetrating' the reality of this experience by grasping the moment in the patient's behaviour at which the decisive intuition of certainty or the suspensive ambivalence of action forces itself upon him, and by discovering the form in which this moment is affirmed through our assent.

One can see the importance that the lived mode of the temporal perspective can have in this formal determination.

A fine example of the analytic value of such a method is given by M. Minkowski (252–71) in a remarkable study of 'a case of pathological jealousy based on mental automatism', republished here from *Annales médico-psychologiques* of 1929. There is no more ingenious and convincing demonstration of the role
111 of the formal mould played by the 'generating disorder' (here primarily the symptom known as 'transitivism') in the morbid passionate contents (feelings of love and, above all, jealousy) and in their obvious disinsertion from both internal reality and object reality.

This brilliant observation should convince us that one cannot understand the true signification of a morbid passion, inadequately indicated by a framework arising from common experience (jealousy), without penetrating into its structural organization.

All the more regrettable is the fact that M. Minkowski takes such care to exclude as artificial all developmental [*génétique*] understanding by way of the subject's affective history from the explanation of such a case. The most sympathetic of his readers can but be struck in the case reported here by the significant alignment between the traumatic memories of childhood (elective libidinal trauma at the anal stage and affective fixation to the sister), the reactivating trauma of adolescence (the man she loves marries one of her friends) and the modes of affective identification in the form of fausse reconnaissance and transitivism, which cause her both to feel depersonalized vis-à-vis the women of whom she is jealous and to believe in the existence of homosexual relations between her husband and his lovers. It is even more striking to see the emergence of childhood memories into consciousness coincide with a relative calming of her problems.

Moreover, because of his openly hostile position regarding psychoanalysis, M. Minkowski aims to establish a new theoretical dualism in contemporary psychiatric research, a dualism that would supposedly update the outdated opposition between organicism and psychogenesis, a dualism that would oppose structural subduction, which he regards as autonomous 112
to the point of speaking of phenomena of 'phenomenological compensation', on the one hand, to the genesis he calls 'ideo-affective', which is that of complexes as defined by psychoanalysis, on the other.

An opposition that is so mutually exclusive can only be sterile.

In a recent work I have myself attempted to demonstrate, in the typical complex of object conflict (the 'triangular' position of the object between the 'you' and the 'me'), the common measure between form and content in what I call 'paranoiac knowledge'.

Equally, I do not believe that man's destination to 'manipulate solids' is what essentially determines the substantialist structure of his intelligence. This structure appears to be tied, rather, to the affective dialectic that leads him from an egocentric assimilation of his milieu to sacrificing his ego to the person of the other. The determining value of affective relations in the mental structure of objects, then, goes far. In my view, the elucidation of these relations has to be pivotal for a just appreciation of the features of lived time in morbid structural types. An isolated consideration of these features does not make it possible, it seems to me, either to record them all or to differentiate them. Hence the somewhat disparate function of the various disturbances in intuiting time in the nosographic entities, where they are studied in this work: here, this function is apparent in consciousness and described as a subjective symptom by the patient suffering from it; while there, it is deduced as structural in the disorder that expresses it very indirectly (melancholia).

The only thing that appears fundamental and, without any doubt, destined to add to the clinical picture of essential dis-
113 criminations, is the subduction of lived time in depressive states; one can, as of now, declare that these states are enriched by a number of structural types (pp. 180–93, 306–27).

Furthermore, one cannot but be thankful to M. Minkowski for having demonstrated the analytic richness of the entity, above all structural, introduced by Clérambault by the name of mental automatism. The significance of the fine work of this master goes well beyond demonstrating the truth of 'organicism', to which he himself seems to have wanted to reduce it and to which a number of his students still limit it.

In this work of science – which is a joint task – M. Minkowski is, furthermore, keen to pay homage to each of those whose views appear to him to make a contribution to the exploration of lived time in the mentally ill [*psychopathes*]. We benefit from very fine expositions of works by Mme Minkowska, M. Franz Fischer, MM. Straus and Gebsattel, M. de Greef and by M. Courbon. Perhaps the ensemble loses in demonstrative value what it thereby gains in richness, and the concept [of lived time] becomes all the more robust as the disorders of lived time are too incidental in character in morbid mental structures to be used otherwise than as secondary in a natural classification of these structures (cf. the brief chapter titled: 'Some Suggestions on the Topic of Manic Excitation' [294–6] and compare it with Binswanger's major study of the *Ideenflucht* published in *Archives Suisses*).

It remains the case that the attention of psychiatrists in clinical contact with patients is hereby called upon to investigate further the nature and variety of these disturbances of temporal intuition.

By integrating their perspective into a full analysis of structures, the future will reveal their true place in the entire range
of forms of mental subduction, the study of which has to be a 114
foundation for modern anthropology.

Moreover, this anthropology cannot culminate in a positive science of the personality. The typically developmental phases of the latter as much as its noetic structure and moral intentionality have to be provided by a phenomenology, as I myself affirmed at the relevant time. M. Minkowski is thus well founded in having sought the categories of his structural investigation in a phenomenological analysis of lived time.

Ever since the term 'phenomenology', originating in Germany, or at least the technical meaning under which it occupies a place in the history of philosophy, was freed of the rigorous conditions of the Husserlian *Aufhebung*, it has come to cover many 'comprehensive' speculations.

Moreover, ever since the term was admitted into France at the level of one of those currencies that provide no guarantee of the exchange that each term of the philosophical vocabulary constitutes – at least for as long as it is living – its use has remained marked by the utmost uncertainty.

M. Minkowski's work aims to stabilize this use, but in the practical mode of Bergsonian intuitionism. Understand by this that it is less a question of doctrinal conformism than of an attitude that is, I would say, almost that of an irrationalist banality whose formulas strike me as somewhat obsolete, just as the academic antinomies of reason on which they feed relentlessly (cf. the chapter on 'succession', etc. [25–34]) seem rather pedantic.

A very personal apprehension of lived duration finds expression underneath this apparatus. It results in an extraordinarily
115 subtle dialectic, the crucial requirement of which appears to be discord and discursive dissymmetry for every antithesis of lived experience – a dialectic that leads by elusive syntheses from vital *élan*, the first direction singled out in becoming, to personal *élan*, correlative to the work, and to *ethical action*, the endpoint, but whose essence, however, remains fully inherent in the very structure of the future (cf. pp. 120–1).

Moreover, this *élan*, which is purely formal and yet the creator of all vital reality, is for M. Minkowski the form of the lived future. This intuition dominates the entire structure of the temporal perspective. Restoring the spatial virtuality that, from this perspective, experience reveals to us will be pursued throughout this work. It requires the enriching intrusion into becoming of ontological couples, 'being one or many', 'to be an elementary part of a whole', 'to have a direction', in order for the creation of the *principles* whose irrationalism, duly regulated from the outset, serve as their civil status: *principle of continuity and succession, principle of homogenization* and *principle of fractionation and continuation* (25–43). In truth, the fissure, although fundamental, in such an irrational deduction appears at the junction between the vital *élan* and the personal *élan*, which requires, or so it seems, the addition of a concrete, intentional given that here is absolutely misrecognized. The attempt, which is not even disguised, to extract from a pure, existential intuition both the *superego* and the *unconscious* of psychoanalysis, which are

'levels' undeniably linked to the social relativity of personality, strikes me as challenging. It looks like the work of a sort of philosophical *autism*, the expression of which has to be taken here
as a datum that is itself phenomenologically analysable, just as 116
the grand systems of classical philosophy can be. The exclusion of all *knowledge* [*savoir*] from the lived reality of duration and the formal genesis of the first empirical certainty in the idea of death, of the first memory in remorse and of the first negation in memory are so many marvellous intuitions, which better express the highest moments of an intense spirituality than the facts immanent in the time that 'one' lives.

I am alluding here to one of the familiar references in the philosophy of Heidegger, and certainly the ideas of that philosophy that have become breathable through the filter of an abstruse language and international censure have left us with demands that I find poorly met here. In a note on p. 18, M. Minkowski declares that he was unaware of this author's thought when his own had already taken definitive form. Because of the exceptional situation in which his dual culture (since, as he insists here, he wrote his first works in German) places him, it is regrettable that we are not indebted to him for introducing the huge amount of work of elaboration achieved by German thought in recent years.

Just as a less systematic misrecognition of Freud would not have censored 'resistance' from the group of his fundamental intuitions, so even the basic aspects of Heidegger's teaching would have induced him to include 'boredom', or at least not to have rejected it out of hand as a negative phenomenon. The very seductive remarks on forgetting, understood as a fundamental feature of the phenomenon of the past, also strikes me as too systematically opposed to the best confirmed clinical data
of psychoanalysis. Lastly, the concept of the *promise*, a real piv- 117
otal point of personality which is meant to present itself as its guarantee, strikes me as too misrecognized, as too absolute to

authenticate personal *élan* solely through the unpredictability and irreducible unknown of its object.

However, so many biases produce some admirable, partial analyses. The original concept of waiting as the authentic antithesis of activity (instead of passivity, 'as our reason might suggest' [87]) is both ingenious and a requirement of the system. The phenomenological structure of desire is highlighted well in the [concept of the] mediate degree of relations with the future (92–100). We are given a masterpiece of insight, lastly, in the analysis of prayer: and this is undoubtedly the key to the book, the book of a spiritual man all of whose effusion seeps into a dialogue that could not be expressed outside secrets of the soul. Let no dogmatic inquisition attempt to track down its postulates: to questions on the nature of the interlocutor, he would answer as he does to questions on the meaning of life and questions on the meaning of death: 'There are perhaps even problems which demand to be lived as such, without their solution consisting in a precise formula' (111) and: 'I would almost like to say: if there is really nothing after death, that remains true only so long as one holds this truth in himself, only so long as one jealously guards it at the base of one's being' (142).

We are fully in the realm of confidences; such confidences are, however, avowals. At a time when the human spirit is happy to affirm the determinations that it endlessly projects into the future, not in the form, criticized here, of expectation [*prévision*], but in the active [*animatrice*] form of the
118 *program* and the *plan*, this 'jealous' withdrawal is distinctive of a vital attitude. It cannot, however, be radically individual, and the 'confidences' in the following chapter turns out to be confessions: the radically vanishing trace of *ethical action* on the tapestry of becoming and the assimilation of *evil* to *the work* (115) refer us to the arcane meditations of a Luther or a Kant. Who knows where the author is taking us, perhaps even further? The last soul of this long hymn to love which the

illumined eye 'scrutinizes' incessantly, of this long appeal to 'go right to the end' that returns on every page, and of this cherished enigma: 'If only we knew what is meant by "rise above"!' (95 and passim) is presented to us by the *élan* that motivates the entire book, should one finally manage to apprehend it in a single glance.

It is not one of the least paradoxes of this long attempt at despatializing time, which is always distorted by measurement, that he is only able to proceed by using a long series of spatial metaphors: '*unfolding*', '*super*-individual character', '*dimension in depth*' (65), '*expansion*' (84), 'void' (85), 'further on' (95), '*radius* of action' (97) and, above all, '"*horizon*" of prayer' (103ff). This paradox is disconcerting and irritating up until the final chapter, which gives the key to it in the form of the intuition, the most original one in the book in my opinion, even if barely outlined, at the end, of another space than geometrical space, namely, the opposite of open space as the framework of objectivity: the *dark space* of fumbling about, of hallucination and music. Compare it to astonishing cries such as this (63): 'A prison, were it identical with the universe, is intolerable to me.' I believe we can say without exaggeration that we are transported to the 'night of the senses', to the 'dark night' of the mystic.

The ambition, enigmatic for the reader at first, on examina- 119
tion proves to be one of ascesis; the work's ambiguity, that of the nameless object of intuitive knowledge.

Hallucinations and Delusions 121

REVIEW OF HENRY EY, *HALLUCINATIONS ET DÉLIRES*,
PUBLISHED IN *ÉVOLUTION PSYCHIATRIQUE*, 1935

There is a fairly large public that suspects that in France the small size of the circles in which current psychiatric research is undertaken cannot be attributed merely to the propaedeutic requirements and esoteric technique justified by the demands of a new order of knowledge. On the contrary, we are dealing with a feature that is too unusual in comparison with the manifest activity in other countries for one not to seek its cause in cultural and social contingencies, which, moreover, are fairly clear, and in the absence of which it would be necessary to raise this feature to the dignity of a positive phenomenon: namely, and speaking plainly, a dearth of inspiration. The public will be convinced that this is not at all the case when, through this small book intended for its use, it comes into contact with a mind whose work, spread across articles and collaborative works, could until now only make its importance and originality known to the initiated.

Henri Ey has not sought to give a summary here of his research on hallucinations. The scale and heterogeneity of this problem have imposed on him a methodical programme of investigation and exposition whose elaboration in his previous work has been pursued with a rare coherence. His research is far from complete in its totality. This new work is merely a 122
moment, but its value is exemplary as much for the research

method as for the theoretical foundations adopted by the author in a field that has already been explored. This is because the hallucinatory phenomena studied here provide through their properties a veritable case demonstration of the author's thought. They are the psychomotor *hallucinations* identified by Séglas in 1888.

Prior to the work I am analysing, it is worth remarking, with Henri Ey, and consistent with the preliminary observations that this analysis led me to make, that 'the history of ideas on psychomotor hallucinations begins and ends with Séglas' (45). This is not to say that this history has stagnated into a professorial stereotype; on the contrary, the development of Séglas's profoundly subversive theories displays the marvels of a mind that not only knew how to 'see new facts' (which would not have been possible without an initial theoretical elaboration), but also, in the preferred contact [*commerce*] he maintains with the object of his discovery, reworks in stages and almost despite himself the mental framework in which he first observed it. We light upon a fine example here of this reciprocal transmutation of object and thought that, as the history of science shows, is identical to the very progress of knowledge.

H. Ey first sets out the stages in the thought of Séglas, which culminates in a 1913 article with Barat and in its final form in a 1914 lecture in which H. Ey recognizes everything essential to his own position, and which his own work only aims to develop further. This lineage [*filiation*] receives the blessing of
123 the Master himself, who had withdrawn into retirement at the time and emerged in order to generously preface this book.

The substance of the latter bears witness to the value of the historical knowledge of ideas, which Ey loves to engage with. This knowledge, productive in any science, is even more so in psychiatry. It would be pointless to want to oppose it to the clinical reality that it helps us understand, or, even worse, to the simplistic and muddled undertakings that in psychiatry pass for experimental research, perhaps because therein flourish in great numbers those that in any authentic experimental discipline would be relegated to the rank of laboratory boors.

Psychomotor hallucinations make it possible to address the problem that H. Ey places at the centre of his work on hallucinations with an exceptional clarity and resolve it with a specific certainty: Is a hallucination a type of interference [*parasite*] disturbing mental life – a low grade automatism which simulates perception, as in an elementary conception like Clérambault's or a very subtle one like Mourge's? In short, is it an object located in the brain that imposes itself on the subject as an external object? Or rather, is a hallucination an organization of beliefs – an integral part of the disturbed relations between the living being and the external world whose objectivity he never sufficiently acquires for the hallucination not to remain propped up by its vital support? Lastly, is a hallucination the affirmation of reality whereby the disturbed subject defends its newfound objectivity?

Psychomotor hallucinations effectively appear initially – 124
and appeared historically – as containing in their very mode a 'powerful factor of splitting of the personality'. Also, the often observable, because motor, feature of the phenomenon seemed to guarantee the objectivity of the supposedly causal automatism.

But the contradictions in such a conception [of split personality] appear very quickly and appear, no less, as a function of the form specific to psychomotor hallucinations.

First, a phenomenological contradiction appears in the earliest classifications where the most real phenomenon (monologue – verbal impulsions) is regarded as the most hallucinatory. Then there is a clinical contradiction. The adherents of 'pure observation' would do well to consider the extent to which it [this conception] corresponds, just at the right moment, to an incoherent conception of the essence of the phenomenon: on the one hand, the more conviction with which patients refer to their 'splitting', the less automatic and more charged with affective signification the phenomenon seems to the observer, just as we find at the beginning of most phenomena of influence. On the other, when in their final stases they appear to be prey to verbal automatisms (uncontrollable monologues, glossomania), the hallucinatory phenomenon disappears or is replaced by a playful attitude.

Consequently, the essential feature of psychomotor hallucinations, whether true or pseudo-hallucinations, is not to be
125 sought in the automatism, regarded as real by the patients, of the purported kinaesthetic verbal image, but in the disturbances to the fundamental feeling of integration of the personality – feelings of automatism and feelings of influence – by which actual phonatory or synergetic movements of phonation are tinged with a phenomenon experienced as either foreign or imposed. As to the 'powerful factor of splitting of the personality', it is not located in a disturbed kinaesthesia, but in the very structure of the function of language, in its phenomenology, which is always marked by a duality, whether it is a case of commanding, deliberating or recounting.

That is the critical movement that unifies the various chapters into which, in part one of this work, H. Ey divides the very extensive knowledge on which he bases his argument: (i) the introduction, which is a recap, in its dialectical place, of the general critique of the concept of automatism in psychopathology that the readers of *Évolution psychiatrique* can find in the third issue of 1932; (ii) an account of the theoretical progress of Séglas's thought, which has the value of a privileged clinical experience; (iii) a review of the current state of the scientific revolution regarding the psychology of imagery and its repercussions for the theory of movement and for the theory of language; (iv) semiology of psychomotor hallucinations; (v) analytic reduction of the latter to imposed phenomena and foreign phenomena; (vi) genetic reduction to feelings of influence and automatism and their conditions.

This first part only acquires its full significance, however, on reading the second. In the latter, H. Ey effectively reintegrates psychomotor hallucinations into mental structures and
delusional behaviour from which, as he shows, they cannot be 126
separated. He describes, in the very evolution of delusions, the favoured stages of their appearance and describes in concrete terms the degree of relaxation and the extent of integrity of the personality that are required for the phenomenon to occur. Lastly, he attempts a natural classification of clinical types in which the phenomenon is to be met with, while at the same time itemizing a number of its aetiological types.

This is, in my opinion, the most valuable part of the book and I can only refer the reader to it in order to benefit from the very rich experience with patients it demonstrates.

If, in effect, everything in this book converges on the patient's reality, it's because everything starts from there. 'It is through contact with mental patients that I have been able to acquire', the author writes, 'some thoughts about hallucinations. If this is a method prejudicial to the understanding of these phenomena, [then] it is clear that all my studies are tainted at the root and signify strictly nothing' (168).

H. Ey knows what questions the nature and conditions of hallucinatory *aesthesia* and the value and mechanism of its features of *exteriority* raise for psychologists and physiologists. It is for this reason that he is also aware that these questions cannot resolve the problem of our patients' hallucinatory *reality*.

It is paradoxical – and to be honest a little comical – to see the very ones who appeal to pure clinical experience take as a given from the start of the problem of hallucinations precisely those psychological qualities whose content is the most uncertain, and base them on the patients' assertions accepted in their
raw state. These supposed clinicians thus become abstractors 127

of delusions and are led to misrecognize a mass of significant features of patients' behaviour and of the progress of their illness. The hybrid nosological entity of chronic hallucinatory psychosis (still currently used in backward circles) alone suffices to demonstrate this. With the clinically very convincing manner in which H. Ey dismantles this entity, he demonstrates that there is no good clinical theory without a healthy critique of the way the phenomena are organized. For reasons identical to the very conditions of knowledge, anyone who claims not to understand such a critique has not succeeded in doing without it; they resort, whatever resources they might have, to a particular critique, but an unsound one.

Pathology of belief – such is the essence, then, of chronic hallucinatory delusions. The ambiguity that both *aesthesia* and *exteriority* display in psychomotor hallucinations has produced, for M. Ey, a particularly favourable case for demonstrating that the essential feature of hallucinations is the belief in their *reality*.

The number of errors that this work strives to dispel justifies its polemical stance. My approbation has perhaps led me to accentuate the tone of my analysis. This interpretation is deliberate on my part and it takes away any right I have to make quarrel with the author in wishing that he had further developed two positive points in his presentation. The first regards the mechanism that produces psychomotor hallucinations: this is the double phenomenological bond that appears to be demonstrated, on the one hand, between belief in their exteriority and the deficit of thought [*déficit de la pensée*] that becomes
128 apparent in their framework, and, on the other, between belief in their validity and the sthenic emotion that accompanies them. The author might perhaps have established these links better if he had addressed the problem of automatic writings, regarding which I have myself had occasion to be struck by. The second point regards the concept, dear to me, of the mental

structure that unifies all forms of chronic delusion and is characteristic of both their elementary manifestations and overall behaviour. Using it systematically in the description of the different types of delusions referred to here might perhaps have led, in the majority of cases, to dissolving psychomotor delusions into delusional mentality more fully.

References

Abasia in a Woman Traumatized by War
Trénel and Jacques É.-L. Lacan are listed as the authors of the original publication, 'Abasie chez une traumatisée de guerre', *Revue neurologique* 1 (1928), Masson, Paris, pp. 233–7. The paper was presented by Marc Trénel and Jacques É. L. Lacan to a meeting of the Société de Neurologie de Paris on 2 February 1928.

Simultaneous Madness
Henri Claude, P. Migault and J. Lacan are listed as the authors of the original publication 'Folies simultanées', *Annales médico-psychologiques* [A.M.P.], no. 1 (December 1931), Masson, Paris, pp. 483–90.

Structure of the Paranoiac Psychoses
'Structure des psychoses paranoïaques' by Jacques Lacan, Intern of the Asiles de la Seine, was published in *La Semaine des Hôpitaux de Paris* (July 1931), pp. 437–45.

'Inspired' Writings: Schizography
J. Lévy-Valensi, P. Migault and Jacques Lacan are listed as the original authors of 'Écrits "inspirés": Schizographie', *Annales médico-psychologiques* [A.M.P.], no. 5 (December 1931), Masson, Paris, pp. 508–22.

The observation this work was based on was presented on 21 May 1931 to a meeting of the Société médico-psychologique under the title: 'Troubles du langage écrit chez une paranoïaque présentant des éléments délirants de type paranoïde (schizographie) [Disturbances of written language in a paranoiac presenting with delusional elements of a paranoid type (schizography)]'.

The Problem of Style and the Psychiatric Conception of Paranoiac Forms of Experience
'Le problème du style et la conception psychiatrique des formes paranoïaques de l'expérience' by Dr Jacques Lacan was published in issue no. 1 of the journal *Le Minotaure* in June 1933, Albert Skira, Paris, pp. 68–9.

Motives of Paranoiac Crime: the Papin Sisters' Crime
'Motifs du crime paranoïaque: le crime des sœurs Papin' by Jacques Lacan was published in nos. 3/4 of the journal *Le Minotaure* in December 1933, Albert Skira, Paris, pp. 25–8.

Psychology and Aesthetics
'Psychologie et esthétique' is a clinical and critical analysis by Jacques M. Lacan of Eugène Minkowski's *Le temps vécu. Études phénoménologiques et psychopathologiques* – a 400-page work in the series, *Évolution psychiatrique*. Lacan's review was published in *Recherches philosophiques*, issue no. 5, 1936, pp. 424–31. [There is an English version of Minkowski's book: *Lived Time: Phenomenological and Psychopathological Studies*, trans. by Nancy Metzel with a new foreword by Dan Zahavi (Evanston, Ill: Northwestern University Press, 2019).]

Hallucinations and Delusions

'Hallucinations et délires' is a clinical and critical analysis by Jacques M. Lacan of *Hallucinations et délire*, a single volume work of 178 pages by Henri Ey, published in 1935 by F. Alcan, Paris. Lacan's review was published in *Évolution psychiatrique*, issue no. 1, 1935, pp. 87–91.